I0532207

*The truest blessing is to live forever not in your body
but in the minds and the hearts of others.*

May He Bless My Name

by Carla M. Cherry

iiPUBLISHING

May He Bless My Name
Copyright © 2024 by Carla M. Cherry

Copyright notice
All rights reserved. No part of this book may be
reproduced in any form or by any electronic or mechanical means, including information
storage and retrieval systems, without permission in writing from the author or publisher,
except for the use of brief quotations in a book review.

Cover design by tonii

ISBN: 979-8-9850204-7-2

Printed in the United States of America

iiPUBLISHING
New York, NY
www.toniiinc.com

For my family and my legacy.

Acknowledgements

The original versions of "We Three Were Water," "Us," and "Psalm 5 for Black Boys" were published by *Raising Mothers*.

The original versions of "Choices," "Worse Than Sticks and Stones," and "With Good Fortune" appeared in *One Art*.

The original version of "A Different Beast" was published in the Garden of Neuro's anthology, *The Talk: Delicate Conversations by Families of Color*.

CONTENTS
PART I

FIRST, THERE WAS LOVE

A SEED IS PLANTED

NEW LIFE

PART II

THE FIRST YEAR

PART III

PART IV

THE MOTHER LEARNS AS SHE TEACHES

STAND

PART V

PART VI

JEJUNITY

THE EMERGING MAN

PART VII

WHY DIDN'T YOU TELL ME?

NO!

DON'T GO!

We Three Were Water

July 13, 2013

I.

Before today's protest at Union Square about Trayvon,
I send one of the coordinators a Facebook message:
"My son wants to attend the march you announced.
Under the circumstances I do not want him to go.
Terrified for him, living in Amerikkka."

Please let him come, he writes. *Please.*
Does your son do any public speaking?
He should speak today for a few minutes about what he is feeling.

I reply:
"He is 19 and swears he is going despite my objections.
How do I know the NYPD won't crack heads?
I am so scared.
Black people aren't respected anywhere.
I am a black mother of a son.
Don't know what to do anymore."

He does not answer.
What reassurance could he, a Black man, offer anyway?
My mother, my sister, and I surround Khari as he laces his sneakers.

"No! Don't go," we cry.
The cops are already feeling some type of way."

We three were water, corroding his steely will.

II.

Children younger than Khari,
the sons and daughters of our foreparents,
had their own D-Day, May 2, 1963.

Four thousand Black youth in Birmingham,
knowing they could be arrested,
marched out of their segregated high schools.

Congregated at Sixteenth Street Baptist Church
before they marched downtown,
and bullies with badges and biting dogs
and fire hoses knocked them down,
and arrested them by the hundreds.
Birmingham desegregated.
Addie Mae, Cynthia, Carole, and Carol Denise,
victims of vengeance.

College students sat straight-backed and still,
at segregated lunch counters
while bigots shouted,
poured drinks or ketchup on top of them,
pushed them off their chairs.

Freedom Riders signed their last wills and testaments
before they boarded the buses.

The parents of Dorothy Counts
pulled her out of Harry Harding High School
after four days of screaming mobs,
rocks thrown, and landing mostly at her feet,
boys spitting in her food at lunch, and
the white girls forced to withdraw offers of friendship.

At least the Counts had let their daughter try.

III.

With George Zimmerman free,
America has neither eyes nor ears for a Black mother's heartache,
will not avenge our rage if a baton
bashes Khari in the head, across his back or legs,
apply salve to soothe his wrists if he is handcuffed.
So, we shackle him with our words and fears.

I have so often seen black and white photos of black men carrying signs--
I Am A Man.
Khari was declaring the same.

Who was I raising him to be?

PART I

FIRST, THERE WAS LOVE

In the Beginning

Daddy picks up Wally and Mommy
from Wally's house off Bruckner Boulevard.
Drives them to the party in Westbury.

Records spinning.
Daddy invites Mommy to dance.

Are you going with anybody?
He asks Mommy for her number.

She is shy.
Daddy calls her twice,
charms her into a Nancy Wilson concert.

He wears a sports jacket.
She usually sews her clothes, but that night,
she wears a white blouse,
red linen miniskirt, and low heels
from Bloomingdale's.

"They had some nice stuff back then," she says now.
My mini skirt wasn't like the ones they have now where you can see every
crease."

Mommy in a mini skirt?
This woman, who only wore A-line skirts and dresses all my life?

At the concert, she notices a funny odor,
and asks, 'What's that smell?"
Daddy shushes her,
whispers it is marijuana.

Mom and I snicker.
Never touched it myself.
I am as square as my parents.

Did you hold hands?

"No. I don't know. Are you serious?
I'm 82 years old. That was in 1968."

She forgets all that remains of his life before her,
is his photo album from the Air Force.

Did Grandma like him?
What about Uncle Bobby? Uncle Ralph? Uncle Reggie? Uncle Don?

"I don't know. They were probably all in the service at the time.
My mother went to the door when he rang the bell.
She kept looking up and looking up and couldn't see his head."

We laugh. Daddy was 6'3".

Did he bring flowers?
"No."

She pauses.

"One time we were at his parents' house,
and he played Wes Montgomery's *A Day in the Life*,
I loved it so much I had him play it three times."

Did you kiss at the end of your date?
"I guess. I don't know. We didn't do nothing," she says.

Until the wedding night.

I know, I know.

Newbies

Ages seven and four, we ask Mom where babies come from
while she oils us down with glycerin and rose water.

She tells us about sperm and eggs.
"The egg," Donna says. "Does it hatch?" I laugh and laugh.

Daddy's thick green paperback copy of *The Human Body*
is on the low shelf of his bookcase so we can reach it.

Our god-sister Crystal comes for a sleepover.
We three take turns reading the book as we use the toilet.

Mommy and Daddy smirk at the echo of our tittering:
pictures of growing penises, ages 0, 7, 14, 21, 25,

speculation about how big our breasts will get,
how soon hair will surround our vaginas.

Wonder

Even we nerdy fifth-grade girls pass around
Are You There God? It's Me, Margaret at lunch.

"We must, we must, we must increase our
bust!"

We rock back and forth with laughter.
I almost choke on my pizza.

Thank God for Judy Blume.

She helps me understand
why I squeezed my chest with my hands
into the shape of a bosom
when I was eight,
why I twirled in the mirror
with the training bras
Mommy bought when I was nine.

My first kiss,
age ten.
With M, in the backseat.
Soft pressing peck
while our mothers shopped for groceries.

I daydream first dates.

But the afternoon of the bloody mire
when I am twelve–
I cry in Mommy's arms over
the cottony bulk
between my hips,
what must be done each month
with my calendar,
how heavy
boy-crushes have become.

I plead for the backward march of time.

Expectations

I'm sick of New York!

Stalled traffic.
Daddy's deep-brown hands
clamp the steering wheel.
He talks to friends in Denver,
and Virginia, about *possibilities*.
After I my admission
to the Bronx High School of Science,
Daddy dashes his picket-fence,
cul-de-sac dreams.
I give Daddy a poem I wrote in Creative Writing.
He shows it to Judy D. Simmons.
She has potential, Melvin.
I had read so many of her articles in *Essence*.
At her word,
I began to believe.
You should major in English, Daddy says.
He envisions me as a journalist.
Traveling around Africa after college.
Joining a black upwardly mobile networking group.
Going on one of the ski trips advertised in *Black Enterprise*.
Meeting a Howard or Hampton or Morehouse man to marry.
From the time I am nine,
Dr. Gwendolyn Goldsby-Grant's
sexual health column in *Essence*
is propped against my knees
as Mommy crisscrosses my hair into cornrows.
All the nights they find me cross-legged on the sofa,
curled up in bed, a book in my face,
Mommy and Daddy assume
I need no instruction
about the choreography of courtship.
With each tower of spaghetti I build on my plate,
they laugh at what it would take

for my dates to feed me.

Admonition

Before

I leave for college,
our family doctor,
a conscious Black woman
who insists Donna and I
get tested for HIV
so we are safe
and informed,
must have seen
her eighteen-year-old self
as I sit on her examination table.

After

she listens to my heart and lungs,
shows me how to examine my breasts for lumps,
asks her nurse draw my blood,
tells me to eat fresh pineapple
to clear up my skin real pretty,
she waves one manicured index finger.

Don't get pregnant while you're in school.

Bloom

Dignified, intellectual Black women professors
leading most classes.
Spelman is where I need to be,

even though I do not always love
every tradition.

Want to curse out the upperclasswomen who awaken us at 4 a.m.,
march us to Manley to sing the Spelman hymn
until we get it right.

That night in Packard Hall, some of us joke,
I don't need to know that song.
My TUITION makes me a Spelman woman!
High-fives all around.

I tell my advisor Dr. Davis I want
to double major in political science and economics,
minors in history and religion,
study Spanish and French
for a career in international/human rights/civil rights law,
and take piano lessons.

Six classes every semester.
With eighteen other credits,
most days I miss piano with Dr. Joyce Johnson,
and I never practice.

The organ under Dr. Johnson's fingers,
feet in Sisters Chapel--
musical majesty.
I wither in my pew every time.

Days thumbing the card catalog at Woodruff (Club Woody) Library–
then a trek to Georgia State or Emory
when you cannot find the books or periodicals you need.

Dr. Harper's Freshman Comp teaches me everything
I did not know about writing a research paper.
Earned a C in her class,
but every paper after that, As and Bs.

Fastidious notes for every lecture,
and when Nikki Giovanni/Atallah Shabazz/Yolanda King/
Herbert Aptheker/Dr. Ben-Jochannan speak on campus.

With two Southern roommates,
I sometimes slip--
I'm fixna/finna go here/there,
but I promise to never stop slap-boxing my vowels,
New York-style.

The Plays!
The River Niger.
The Death of the Last Black Man in the Whole Entire World.
Boochie.
Flyin' West.
Late Bus to Mecca.

Film festivals!
A Dry White Season.
In case it is of South African origin,
I remove my gold jewelry,
slam it on my desk in solidarity.

The day Nelson Mandela is released from prison,
we watch the news to see him walk freely with Winnie,
waving at the crowds.
That summer, I go to Yankee Stadium to hear him speak.

Farrakhan at the Omni.
Those of you who do things to your hair.
As my relaxer grows out,
I comb tresses into square sections.
Double helix twists.

Nights at Morehouse with my friends.
Spades.
Books: Walter Rodney. Ivan Van Sertima. Paula Giddings.
A party occasionally since I really cannot dance.

Wander the shelves in The Shrine of the Black Madonna's bookstore.
Attend their church some Sundays.
Love the pro-Black message and music.
Join.
A member calls me at least twice a week
to see when I will join a committee and attend meetings.
After weeks of my demurring to study, she scolds,
You have to leave room for God.

I search for other affirming spaces.

Join AST, An African Sisterhood.
Journey. We dress in white. Wrap our hair in matching gelees.
We walk in silence, contemplate ourselves as African descendants.
As women.

After struggling through Econ I,
political science is my major with a minor in history.

Junior year. Con Law.
I have passion for justice, disdain for legalese.

I learn about Umkhonto We Sizwe.
Destabilization of South African liberation movements
during apartheid is my thesis topic.

I write the occasional poem.
A couple are published in *The Spelman Spotlight*.

Open mics at Soul Source Bookstore.

My hands shake less each time I perform.

A SEED IS PLANTED

Destiny

Thin.
Soft-spoken.
Light brown-skinned.
Thin-rimmed glasses.
A small hoop in his left ear.
After he performs his poem,
he announces a poetry group,
Young African Writers Collective.
Invites people to take down his number,
and call if we want to attend.

A couple of weeks later,
I meet him outside the Edgewood MARTA stop.
We sit on the steps.
Knee to knee, we share—

my freeze tag/hopscotch/double-dutch days in New York City.
        He is a Georgia boy, born in Indiana.
        Summers with his father in Germany.
        Our love of books.
        He loves John Updike.
        I love Toni Morrison.

That diagonal shift of his gaze?
Shy, like me.
First few meetings, it is just us two.
Magnetic field
between our eyes, our smiles.
I am a faithful member.

I sit on the floor of his grandmother's basement.
He invites me to sit next to him on the sofa.
His fingers make a pathway
to the underside of my knees.

Kisses.

Blow

Mouths in slow
skids   fingers
map-making
limbs unlocking
and locking
in labor

Train   tunnel

Cooling like
rain   me
ashamed of
the sound
we make
against the floor

We, each
pet the sheet,
to avoid the
passion pond

O, how we
shatter silence

into shards of glass

Plans

My credits for my degree,
my thesis,
completed,
I could have stayed home
after Christmas break.

Not knowing
what to do next with my life,
not ready to spin off
from my college circle,
I return
for spring semester of senior year.

In my free time
I am in a flexuous tangle
with him,
in hip-to-hip
synchronous sway,
hitting guitar riff-high notes—

Sade's "Cherish the Day."

I Want Him To Be My Man

Dinners.
Car rides.

Stirrings of love swim
my chest,
my navel.

I want him to be my man,
but he is seeing another woman.

I swirl.
Focus on the good feels,
until I am convinced I don't mind.

He tells me
when he was younger
he used to break car windows.
When he was in a facility,
he didn't want to be considered a punk.
He picked up a chair
and hit a guy who threatened him.

I curl into this soft of him.

Chance

The night we run out of condoms
he is convinced
he is sober enough

to pull out in time

Addled by attar of the poppy
the draw and suck of the pink lily

it is as if we sit outside
and try to count every star in the sky

Wisp

We four, between 10 and 13 years old,
concrete stoop beneath our denim-clad bottoms,

slurp cherry/orange/lime popsicles,
toss around our dreams for the future like yo-yos.

"Seven!" they exclaim, when I announce
the number of children I want to have.

Girly giggles.

I will go to college, I say,
marry at 22, and soon after,

my husband and I will have a baby
every two years until we achieve my magic number.

We will be young enough to keep up with,
and understand, our

boy, then girl, then girl, then boy,
then boy, then girl, then boy.

They will be fast friends,
book-brilliant,
quick-handed if anyone
bothers their siblings.
We will be done raising them by our mid-fifties.

A big family—
steaming bowls of soul,
laughter around a long dining table.
Somebody close to your age is always around to confide in.

But when I am 21,
in January 1993,
what I want most is for my period to come.

Petition

For all of January,

I flip pages in my calendar.
Hope I circled the wrong December day.

For extra luck,
I stop wearing pads,
alternate my two favorite pairs of jeans.

Beseech God for

       a brook
             or river
                  of blood
                        to ooze
                                gush
                                        spate

                                                a ruinous red stain

In The Light

February 2, 1993.
My not-quite-boyfriend drives us to a free clinic.

The counselor gives me a pregnancy test.
She smiles at us as we wait,
confirms what I know from

       two weeks of cramps,
       pads that remain unstained white.

He smiles back at her.
Holds my hand.

A burst of white light behind my eyes.
At the nape of my neck.

Stirrings of a soul tie.
My hands cradle my belly.

It must be why she says,
I won't show you the video.

I thank her for sparing me gore of shredded fetal limbs.

Despite the days I have cried
in secret
over where and when and how
I will find a job,
where I will live,
how to tell my mother and father,
I know, at that white light,
I am going to keep my baby.

We go to a cafe.
I am smiling.
I wrap a cup of lemony tea and honey

in the womb of my hands.

NEW LIFE

Smacked

At the cafe
our kneecaps kiss
under the table.

Whiz wheel of hope
spins in my chest.

Hold my hand again.
Tell me we three will be a family.

He says
he will send me money,

our child can spend
summers with him,

but he cannot commit
to coupledom.

Pride
compels the corners
of my mouth upward,

beats back the question,
what have I been to you all this time?
coerces an "I understand" aloud.

To the gathering waters
in my eyes
my inner voice commands,

Peace!
Be still.

Normalcy

Swooning, spinning.
I cling to my routines.
As an aspiring teacher, I volunteer
at an all-black elementary school.

Brown hands in the air like Roman candles
through addition, subtraction, fractions, story hour,
this class of second graders loves to hug.

One morning, a burst of blood.
I tell the teacher I have to leave.

Rush to the bathroom.
Stuff my soiled underwear with toilet paper as I cry.
Run to the office.
The principal is on the only phone.
She nods at my whispered request to make a call.
Too ashamed to reveal my emergency,
I quietly squeeze my legs together,
hoping I will not stain the chair as I wait.

God, please let my baby be okay.

When I call my not-quite-boyfriend,
he drives me straight to the hospital.
Trans-vaginal ultrasound.
A threatened miscarriage.

The baby is still in the womb.
Doctor points to the blip onscreen.
Like an apple seed.
Five weeks along, due for October 3.

Were you testing me, little one,
to make sure I want you?

Relief,
like an ocean breeze.

Betrayal

Now I am sitting on the edge
of my 19-year-old sister's bed,

in her Spelman dorm room,
telling her I am going to be a mother.

Donna glares at me.

Her back against the wall,
fat tears in free-fall,

my hands on my navel,
I inhale/exhale a current of calm,

like when we were girls,
staring at the ceiling, terrified of the dark.

Descendant of women
who transformed table scraps
into sumptuousness,
I promise her
I will spawn success
out of this shame

over shattered norms.

Tread

Morning sickness,
a fist to the gut for six weeks.

As baby siphons blood,
readings and papers are not done.
Missed exams.
Magna cum laude status in danger.

I skulk from dorm to cafeteria and back.
Dodge my professors.

Donna tells me Dr. Gomez,
my favorite history professor,
keeps demanding of her,

WHERE is your sister?!?

As my classmates, friends,
stride terra firma:
jobs
international travel
graduate school,

I am sinking
in the downdraft
of this whirlpool
of fear.
Loneliness.

I flail my arms.
Choke.

My baby!
I cannot drown.

I propel myself to the surface.

With strong strokes of purpose, I head downstream.

Dam

Xylecia,
my freshman year roommate,

> born on September 17th
> just like my mother's mother,
> who showed me how to find
> cute clothes at thrift stores,

> who, when I blasted Prince's "Batman" in our room,
> put on a cape and danced around our room
> until I collapsed from laughter,

> who packs us up in her little red Chevy some weekends,
> drives us to Chattanooga
> for her mama's fried whiting
> and sweet potato pie,
> her daddy's monkey bread,
> Lookout Mountain's views
> of Georgia, Kentucky, Virginia,
> South Carolina, North Carolina, and Alabama,

> Sundays of she and her sisters singing
> *Ride On, King Jesus*
> before her father preached,

is the first friend I tell.

In her dorm room, sitting on her bed, I sputter:

I don't want to be a single mother.

She pulls me to her shoulder.

Silently lets me cry.

News

Guess what?
You're going to be a grandmother!

That's not funny.

Mommy hands Daddy the receiver.
He curses when I repeat my news.

Instead of driving
to Maryland and North Carolina
to gather Cousins Maceo and Manson and their bulging fists,
Daddy keeps his promise
to Donna
not to beat
my not-quite-boyfriend down.

He flies down with Mommy that weekend.
When I open my door,
concern engraved on their faces,
I say,
You're late! Come in!
with the snap of February air,
too full to say
how happy I am to see them,
how unworthy I feel of their love.

We go out to eat.
They invite my child's father.
Before dessert,
they ask him to step outside,
tell me to stay put.
Not-quite-boyfriend never returns to the table.

Daddy says,
He has no plan for you.
Nowhere for you to live.

Mommy says, *Come back home.*

Reconciliation

Not-quite-boyfriend invites me
to join a group of friends at a lounge
and listen to jazz.

I agree, hoping to restore some scrap
of what we had been,
for the being in my belly.

He passes me an envelope with
one of Brother Zakee's handcrafted cards.

Red parchment paper, with the Adinkra symbol,
Gye Nyame—
the Supremacy of God-
in a black and gold border.

Inside is a poem
about the richness of the amber
in my eyes,
and
of my soul.

Maybe we can make it work,
I think,
at these hints of divine love,
at the yes in his eyes.

I am overcome by a warmth
like those nights
under a blanket

in his grandmother's basement.

Shelter

I.

Final semester almost over.
I must move out of the dorm.

Not-quite-boyfriend asks his grandmother
if I can move in with them.

She is in Section 8 housing.
A limit on the number of residents, so the answer is no.

No job, no money for a place of my own,
but I do not want to burden my parents' largesse.

A friend of his owns a house in Atlanta,
and invites us to live there.

He has me call the mother of his friend's son
to tell me how she applied for welfare:

*I told my social worker I didn't know the full name
of my son's father. Didn't know where he was.*

I go to the office with the address,
phone number of where we will be living.

My unsmiling social worker
is eight months pregnant.

I lie--my baby's father's name is Kenneth,
and no, I do not know his last name.

So, you don't know his last name at all?

No, I keep saying, cheeks and neck aflame,
cut by sharp edges in her voice.

She punches the number of my soon-to-be-landlord into the phone.
It is a non-working number.

How could my not-quite-boyfriend
send me here so unprepared?

The social worker frowns
as she says I can come back tomorrow

to finish the application

with a valid number for where I will be living.

II.

Back in my room, I stare up at my poster of Malcolm
with his gun peering through the window,

photos of Joie Lee, other beautiful, brown-skinned women
that I cut out from *Essence* and taped to my walls.

Daddy had not worked double shifts,
Mommy had not run through her savings,

so I could live on the same system
she worked to escape right after high school.

I tell the social worker I changed my mind
and will not be completing the application.

I call my parents.
Ask if I can come home.

My mother's sigh before her yes,

is cool breath over coffee.

Oracle

One evening
I am with my sisters.

Nozibele offers me
a reading
of the Metu Neter oracle.

One of her questions:
Are you doing something contrary to your beliefs?

Synchronous
Mmhmmm.

Hands on my shoulders.
Rubbing my back.

She tells me,
you have
high probability
of success.

According to the Metu Neter,
The Way is open.
So much will depend
upon the work that you do.

I begin to ask
what she means by work,
when there is
a bubbling in my belly.

Quickening.

I stroke my linea nigra.

She Wants To Meet The Mother
Of Her Grandchild

His mother invites me to spend the night.
After not-quite-boyfriend goes to bed,
she talks about her marriage to his father.

He wasn't strong enough for me.

Before I go to bed,
she tells me that several years ago,
my-not-quite-boyfriend
was hospitalized for manic depression.

That night,
I rummage our talks,
time spent.

His aggressive driving.
Breaking into cars when he was a teenager.
The assault he fought off.

Was that incident
at a psychiatric hospital?

Oh.
Oh no.
Why didn't he tell me?
Will my baby inherit this illness?

I will watchfully wait.

Nestled

Grandma crochets two blankets for me.
The first made of white yarn,
patches of baby blue,
patches of pink,
the other white,
interweaved with various shades of green and blue.

Algernon's mother
crochets a baby blanket for me also:
white, interlaced with sky blue ribbons—
the colors of Spelman.

Laura, young wife and mother herself,
tells me I can write to her. Commiserate.

Xylecia's father lends me three books
about parenting in the Christian faith.

Her mother talks to me
woman-to-woman,

revealing sticky spots
cracks
along her path to marriage/motherhood.

Cradled in the work,
the caresses
of these hands and hearts,
seeds of courage

bloom like autumn joy.

Dear Oprah,

I.

I suck my teeth when they announce you
as our commencement speaker.

It is your green contact lenses.

Freshman year, my roommates,
tired of my complaining during your shows,
once tried to put me out of our room.

Why weren't your dark brown eyes enough?

I needed you
brash
bold
in your earthshaking brown beauty
like your Sophia.

We could be two cognac diamonds smashing emeralds.

II.

Oprah,

when you were 13,
did you crave the male gaze belonging to
caramel-colored girls
with eyes the color of the Caribbean Sea?

I loved how they braided my hair,
but had little faith in the cooing over me
from pretty-is-as-pretty-does
grandmothers, mother, aunts, big cousins,
when I was frilly and patent-leather clad.

Daddy, Pop-Pop, my uncles.
Sunrays,

moonbeams,
when they called my name.
Saw their even-toothed beautiful smiles in mine, but
I was a girl who thought other people's windows
were better than my mirror.

You got pretty eyes!
Dreamy crooning
to black and brown kids with
blue/green/hazel/light brown
soul-windows.

At night,
I imagine myself
with a thinner nose,
green eyes,
hair like my god-sister Crystal's black silk,
like video models,
low-hanging and swinging.

A book cover at Black Liberation Bookstore–
black girl, downcast eyes
holding a white doll–
beckons me.
The Bluest Eye.

Somebody,
love Pecola.

Say she is pretty.
Save her from her drunk father,
the mother, who never hugged her as hard
as the white children she cleaned after.
Six-fingered Maureen Peal,
light skin and green eyes,
the glory of the room.
I love Claudia and Frieda, the only ones to seethe.

After I close the book, I proclaim Black Beauty

like I was on loudspeaker.
But I did not know how to step out of the shadows of the girls
who had the latest clothes to wear.

When boys that I like do not like me back,

I stumble instead of saunter.
Stub my toes.

III.

Oprah,

In ninth grade,
my best friend Tanya,
deep cocoa brown-skinned,
her thick hair perfectly curled,
sees my beauty when I cannot.

Tells her mother I hide,
keep my coat on in class
even when the heat is on high.

Mrs. Manning brings us into her bedroom.
She looks at Tanya as she says,
Sorry to break your confidence!

Sits in her chair,
crosses her long, elegant legs.
Scolds me.
How dare I doubt God's genius
in how He made me.

When Tanya and I are sixteen,
around her parents' dining room table,
Mr. Manning assures:

Men are going to want smart girls like you.

IV.

See, Oprah?

Had the wisdom all along,
but I have always been a little hardheaded.

Daddy sitting on the floor, back propped against the sofa, watching TV
after a long day of loading baggage on airplanes.

His outstretched legs, my hurdles,
as I run around the living room.

I am 4 years old.

"Stop it, Carla," Mommy warns, busy with baby Donna.

I trip.
Hit my head on that parquet floor.

"Oh, Melvin!" my mother cries.
"She'll be alright," he replies.

She ices my head when a knot takes center stage on my forehead.
The swelling goes down.

A week later, I hop over Daddy's outstretched legs as he watches TV.
I fall.

A knot grows on the same spot.

V.

Oprah,
at the podium on May 16, 1993,
you tell us that every jerk you ever dated
showed you what you didn't want in a man,
and challenge us Spelman women
to *go out there and triumph.*

I clap and cry.

That night in bed,
I watch my abdomen

                              e

                 s

           i

r

                 f

                       a

                            l

                                 l

Sunflowers,
buttercups,
turn themselves towards the sun.

Nobody has to tell a star to shine.

All I had wanted was a man
who dug me enough to play a beautiful song
three times in a row if I asked.

Why had I settled in this gully of expectation,
gravitated to the shade of half-measure—
a not-quite-boyfriend.

In my head, a voice:
Because you did not think you could do any better.

VI.

Junior year, Mom finds out a cousin attends Morehouse.
I call him, and we chat.
He offers to drop by.

In the lobby of McAlpin Hall,
my cousin, over 6 feet,
square-jawed and jock-handsome,
is with three of his friends, who,

      anticipating
      doe eyes
      high fashion
      hair curving, pointing,

at the promise of pleasure,

encircle the front desk like a pack of wolves.

His boys snicker when they see me,
no makeup,
hair brushed back into an Afro puff.

My cousin does not demand they leave,
threaten to rip vocal chords from their throats,
before or after he hugs me.

Sometimes it's hard to believe you are a ruby
when you get hurled like a skipping stone.

Oprah, so many of my Spelman sisters had their look *together*.
I felt like a daisy in a field of roses.

Forgot the verses
about pearls and swine and equal yokes.

And like that four-year-old
with the fat knot on her forehead,
I let a man who did not want a committed relationship
caress me behind my knees.

VII.

Oprah.

Thank you for the affirmation.

Four months pregnant,
I can go home
to my father and my mother who love me,

find a way to clean up the mess
I have made of my life,

assume the crown I was built for.

Split

Thank you, God, for yet another sign
that we are not meant to be,
that on the way to Hartsfield Airport,
when I look to my right,
and wave at my smiling child's father in an adjacent car,
his eyes are fixed on the road,
and he does not see me.

Thank you, Daddy, for your silence,
steady hands on the steering wheel,
straight-ahead stare,
refusal to honk the horn to get his attention,
beckon him to pull over to the shoulder
when I exclaim,
"Look, his car is right next to ours!"

I might have been swayed by the bouquet of flowers,
who even knows what kind,
resting in his passenger's seat.

God, thank you for whatever delays his arrival at our gate,
for preventing anything from postponing our flight back to New York,
and a corny scene of him calling my name,
me craning my neck to find his voice, us running towards
each other, spewing plans to shrink a 900-mile-long chasm
with my new degree, his half-a-job, and a four-month-old fetus between us.

God, I am grateful the flowers go in the trash.

Thank you for the upperclasswomen who awakened us at 4 a.m.
to memorize the lyrics of the Spelman hymn Freshman year:

Standards.
Honor.
Undaunted.
Beacon.
Noble work.

Undersong

I get a job through a temp agency--
riding around with a salesman for Philip Morris.

Every time I hang signs advertising cigarettes
to other brown and black people

in the bodegas of Washington Heights,
my conscience is a hollow of quicksand.

As I near my third trimester
my mother warns me

not to hold my arms above my head,
but I have to when I hang the signs up.

I am terrified the umbilical cord
is wrapping around my baby's neck.

I feel low.
Carry low, too.

Cannot keep straight which gender
that is supposed to be.

People look at my growing belly
tell me girl, tell me boy.

My blood vessels, conduits of ire
at male freedom to walk away.

Just me and my daughter,
is my undersong.

I would guide this girl to womanhood.
Teach her to love herself most of all.

Until my seventh month,
and the sonogram.
Almond-shaped eyes
and a penis.

The technician is out of film,
so I cannot have my baby's ultrasound photo,

but what worries me most is
how toxic has my rage made my womb?

Clear as Water

My Aunt Joan.
In my favorite picture of us,

my tiny hands holding her fingers,
I am straight as a rod

as I practice walking
across Nana and Pop-Pop's sofa.

Presents for our birthdays.
Twin gold angels with bells to hang on our Christmas tree.

When I went natural,
Aunt Joan bought me a jar of Let's Jam

to help me tame the tresses
sprouting from my head like finger grass.

Aunt Joan, so proud of me on graduation day,
had flown down from D.C.

to see me cross the stage in my cap and gown,
her big brother's eldest child,

first of the grandchildren
to earn a college degree.

I wait until my second trimester
to tell her about my pregnancy.

I'm sure Daddy told her before I do.
She acts as if she did not know.

My child's father's abandoned promises?

Aunt Joan says, *You've got bigger fish to fry.*

Choices

A follower of Dick Gregory in the seventies,
Daddy buys a copy of his *Natural Diet for Folks Who Eat*.
On days off, he juices carrots, celery, and apples.
Pours us equally full glasses.
I gulp olive-colored liquid dutifully.
Laugh as Donna sneaks to the bathroom to spit it out.
No more pork, lamb chops, liver with fried onions,
roast beef, or hamburgers.
He takes us with him to the health food store on White Plains Road
to buy multi-vitamins, herbs like goldenseal,
its bitter tea made sweet with raw honey when we are sick.
Donna and I fall in love with carob and Tiger's Milk bars.
Daddy sells Dick Gregory's Bahamian Diet in the eighties.
Even mixed in orange juice, it tastes like chalk,
but I am proud of my path to good health.
When I am seventeen, I read Gregory's book.
Become a vegetarian.
Happily go along with Daddy to Sundial on Boston Road.
Take Woodroot tonic to keep from getting colds.
I point at my pregnant belly and look at Daddy.
My baby will have the best.
Sundial's herbalist sits across from me,
tells me to take a spoonful of olive oil each day.
Omega 3s will strengthen my baby's brain and heart.
I will breastfeed.
Have a natural childbirth.
But when you are poor,
when you ask about
a doula or midwife,
a birthing center,
the doctor scoffs,

"A what?"

Breath

Lamaze with Mommy.
We practice
long breathing
in through my nose,
out through my mouth,
hard exhales
during the contractions—
hee-hee, hoo, hee-hee, hoo—
to keep me from
bearing down,
pushing
before I am supposed to,
and tearing.
My child's father
comes to New York to be present for the birth.
He joins me and Mom in Lamaze.
I am relieved to no longer be
the only mother-to-be without the father.

Evenings, he rests his left hand on my belly
to feel his child's hands and feet.
We go for a walk.
He tells me he wants to marry me.
A ceremony in Atlanta at the Herndon Home.
He tells Daddy and Mommy about our plans.
Their smiles do not disguise *yeah, right* in their eyes.
Two weeks before my due date, he goes back to Atlanta.
Without explanation.

I scratch his name off the Lamaze certificate.
Replace it with Mommy's.
I lean against the back cushions on the sofa.
Peruse my book of African names.
Select my favorites and say them aloud.
Kwesi. Ngai. Bakari. Aiyetoro. Dumisani. Damani.

Watch my son stretch his limbs through the window of my womb.

Break

My baby is two weeks late.
The amniotic fluid is low.

They admit me.
Give me pitocin.

One of the nurses that preps me for inducement
shakes her head.

"They don't want to come into this world."

I want to ask,

Why would you say this to a woman
about to give birth for the first time?

but I press my mouth closed, afraid to anger anyone
assigned to help me through this task.

The enema makes me wonder
if my bowels will ever empty.

Mom helps me wash up as best I can,
then doctor and nurses peer and poke
the undercarriage of me.

Legs spread.
A hand covered by a plastic glove,
index finger wriggles its way into my canal
while I count the spots on the ceiling and try not to cringe.

An amniotic hook.
A rush of fluid against my bottom and legs.
Forceps.
Fetal scalp electrodes.
The beeping and thumping of the fetal monitor.
I try the Lamaze breathing
to get through the contractions.
The Lamaze instructor showed us
how to open the cervix—
on her knees
rocking
moaning
like she was making love.

I cannot raise myself up,
open my mouth to do it.

Grandma, at 19,
birthed her first child at home without anesthesia,
a midwife laying hot towels on her belly
to steam her baby out.

I am not her.
I need something to survive this tug-of-war in my womb.

I want Demerol!

So glad Mommy is by my side,
that she ignored my effort to be strong
and independent when
I said she did not have to finish
the cycle of Lamaze classes.
That she buried her disappointment in me.
She is here to hold my hand
while I slip in and out of consciousness,
cry and call out for
eight hours and fifty-two minutes.

I awaken in time for the rush of bodily flesh and blood.
A light slap.
His cries as they clean him up.

I lift my head, crane my neck,
stretch my arms to reach for my baby.

When they pass him to me, I say, "my son."

With him in my arms, I instantly understand
why lionesses
bare their teeth and growl,
geese congregate and hiss
when their young are approached.

I tuck him in my left arm.
Try to keep still.

I want
to close my legs,
escape the heat of the overhead lamp,
the sound of clicking metal.

Episiotomy,
the doctor laments.

I mumble something to my mother.
Pass my son to the nurse.

Fall asleep.

PART II

THE FIRST YEAR

us

At the nursery
one of the nurses is surprised to see me.
You're walking around?
God Bless you!
I sit with my son in the rocking chair.
Caress his skin, his fists, his feet.
His pale skin has undertones of yellow
like the inside of a chestnut.
Search for, find me,
in the curve of his eyes.
Survey skin
around the beds of his fingernails
to guess how brown he will become—
a dark cashew.
Cannot afford the naming ceremony
with family and friends I wanted
so in that rocking chair
in the crook of my left arm
I whisper his name
in his right ear three times.
(   )born on a Tuesday
Khari: kingly
(   ) blessing
Knowing his first name will be mangled by many tongues,
I choose his second name to be first on the birth certificate.
I sing Bob Marley's *Three Little Birds*

until he falls asleep.

Milk

Lift my son out of his bassinet.
Sit with him on the chair by my hospital bed.

Pull my breast out of my hospital gown.
Try to place my left nipple in his mouth.

It goes flat.
He fusses, wriggles his hands for twenty minutes.

I want my mother,
but
Ew, Mom answered, then shivered,
when I asked about breastfeeding.
I gave you both the bottle.

Too ashamed to call Grandma,
Aunt Verne, Cousin Saundra, Aunt Joan,
to help me do this simple, natural thing.

After I sign the paperwork for his birth certificate,
the social worker's eyes well up at
me struggling,
son squirming.

She tries to help,
her arm under mine,
as I offer the right nipple,
then the left again.

I shift on the chair,
lift my weight off the stitches
pulling my vaginal wall back together.

The nurse.

A bottle.
Blood abandons my stomach.

Not formula!
Breast is best!

My son shivers as she cradles him.
She listens to his heart.

What's wrong with him?
What's wrong with me?

When she brings a bottle,
I let her let him drink.

Later that night
when they bring our meals

they serve sparkling cider
to us new mothers.

On the other side of the curtain,
my Nigerian roommate's husband sings,

Daddy's girl, Daddy's girl.

I bury my face in a white bath towel.
Soak it silently.

The other mothers eat, and

clink glasses with their husbands.

Meanwhile

Mommy

stocks the beige dresser:
bibs and blankets,
washcloths and towels,
onesies,
shirts,
pants and socks,
groups of three
in each drawer

while

Daddy
flips the instructions back and forth,
rifles through his toolbox
builds the matching crib.

Mom lines
the bars of the crib
with the baby bumper.

Covers the mattress with the pad and linens.
Lays out the matching comforter,
tucks the ends.

They attach the mobile to the crib.
Turn it on.
Watch it slowly spin 360 degrees.
Listen to xylophonic lullaby.

Imagine their newborn grandson sound asleep.

They hold hands and pray.

Snip

Forty-eight hours to decide.
I would not consider this if I'd had a girl.
The few I have seen, have been circumcised.
I am too shy to ask Daddy if he had been.
I read that circumcisions prevent the growth of smegma. STDs.
I want optimal health for my son.

I hope Khari forgives me.

I did not know smegma was harmless.
Looks like pearls.
When they bring him to me, penis bandaged,
a typhoon of regret storms my chest.
Too late for me to say, *Teach me how to pull back the foreskin.*
I would have reminded him every day.
If the foreskin separated,
I would have learned how to teach him to retract it.

I hope Khari forgives me.

I follow after-care instructions to the letter.
No diaper wipes. Khari waves his arms and legs
as I cleanse him with gentle pats of soapy water.
I stare at the glans. Like a tiny mouth.
I imagine it whispering,
Do you know what you're doing?

I hope Khari forgives me.

Home

I lie on my right side on the sofa
with Khari in the crook of my arm.

My favorite second mother, Mrs. Carroll,

> who never held back a thought,
> who babysat Donna and me,
> fed us treats from her uber-clean kitchen,
> whose husband Mr. Carroll smiled
> whenever we were around
> and that was an accomplishment,
> because like she said,
> he didn't like *nobody*,

walks over to the sofa,
leans on her cane,
peers at Khari,
and smiles.

"He looks like something, don't you know.
So many newborn babies just look a mess."

I look down at my son's clearly formed
eyes, nose, and mouth.

Whisper a thank you to God.
Smile up at Mrs. Carroll and Mom.
Pray that I parent even half as well as they.

The phone rings and Mom rises to answer.
It is Aunt Joan.

Mom weeps.
Aunt Joan has lymphatic cancer.

I cradle Khari, begin to cry.

Bigger fish to fry.

Awe

One morning
as he sleeps
in my arms
Khari rests
his face
on his left hand
as if
he is thinking.
I rush
over to Mom.
Mommy, look!
Quick!
Take a picture!
She does,
and we stare
in silence
afraid to disturb
this melody
of quiet.
I lift Khari
to my face
and inhale.
When I have
the money,
I will buy
a bouquet
of gypsophila
each year.
Relive the sweetness

of baby's breath.

First Look

Khari's father comes to New York to meet his son.

He gives me new a teapot and
a white and pink mug that says *Mom*.

I take him by the hand.
Lead him upstairs.

He lifts Khari out of his crib.
Sits on my bed.
Peers down at him.

He's got a turkey neck,
he laughs.

"He does not!",
I snap,
while I retrieve *my* beautiful sleeping son.

I,
who saved scrub cap,
hospital ID bracelet,
a lock of Khari's hair,
an orange leaf from our first walk outside
for his baby book,

look down at Khari,
silently apologize that his father
is not like mine,
who hoped his firstborn
would be a boy
named Russell;

who looked down at newborn me,
named me after Carla Thomas.
So brown, so elegant.

Something Good

Berceuse

I.
Who will be his pediatrician?
Dr. Hall, I say.
Oh, they reply.
Is he good? I ask.
He's OK. We're better.

I stare at these two white doctors, wondering if they are joking, and if they are, they do not respect new mothers if they think it is funny to make them doubt the competency of their child's pediatrician. What is it that inspires their derision, their hubris? Dr. Hall's medical schooling at the University of the West Indies? Small office? His Blackness?

II.
On the day of Khari's first check-up,
Dr. Hall gently lays Khari on the examination table.

Khari's gaze
follows Dr. Hall,
his stethoscope,
as he leads it from his chest to Khari's,
leans in
for rate and rhythm of his heart valves.

Khari gurgles.
Joy.
To be a black boy in this arch of safety.

How was your labor? Delivery?
he asks, as he lays Khari in the cradle of his scale.
The lilt of Jamaica unwrinkles my brow.

"It was normal.
Khari was 7 pounds, 7 ounces. 20 and a quarter inch long."

Today he is 9 pounds, 10 ounces, and 22 and a quarter inch long.

Khari is healthy.
Dr. Hall becomes my voice of reason in this season of new motherhood.

When it looks like Khari has a heartbeat in his head,
I ask,

Why is his head throbbing?
What is that dent?

Dr. Hall lays his hand on Khari's head.
A blessing.

He looks at me and smiles.

His fontanelle.
His skull is leaving room for his brain to grow.

Oh.
What is all this dry flaking on his head?

Cradle cap.
I learn to shrug and brush it away.

When Khari's cough sounds like a puppy's bark,
It's just colic.

Dr. Hall tells me to make a steam room:
run the hot water in the shower full blast,
sit with Khari until the walls sweat,
and hot air clears his lungs.
It works.

What about vitamins?

You don't need to give those to him.
Just feed him a well-balanced diet.

Dr. Hall,
his heart, his hands,

guardian to my miracle of blood and bone.

Daddy Taught Us To Read Road Maps

but he also said,

Always look for landmarks.

During our driving lessons, I learned to look for

large clocks on buildings
parks
houses with unusual colors
anything to guide me through the unfamiliar.

Mom taught us to kneel each night,
pray the Lord will keep our souls,
take them if we fail to wake.

Sunday school with best friends Niecy and Tonya.
My favorite hymn is "Praise Him."
Days sitting on my bed,
legs folded underneath,
big book of Bible stories on my lap,
David slays mighty Goliath with a rock.
Jochebed sets Moses in the basket of reeds.

In this North American Wilderness,
Whom shall I turn to?
Whom shall I fear?

One second Sunday,
I dress Khari all in white.
Shirt. Pants. Socks. Shoes. Cap.

We

Me
Khari
Daddy
Mommy
Donna
Aunt Verne
Cousins Darryl
Kiameshia
and Eric, one of his two godfathers

gather at Abyssinian Baptist Church.

After Reverend Butts announces Khari's name and mine,
he takes Khari in his hands,
raises his arms 90 degrees,
turns in a slow circle.

I look up.

Whom shall I turn to
in this North American wilderness,
with so much to fear?

I survey
smiling faces of my family

hundreds looking down
murmuring approval.
Applause.

Sunlight streaming into sanctuary is manna.
Reverend Butts passes Khari back to me.

"Let the church say amen," he commands.

Amen.

Worse Than Sticks and Stones

A childhood friend tells me,
Now you're just another statistic.

That phrase,
an earworm.
It wiggles.
Writhes.
Burrows.

Swindels me out of new mom pride.

When I go to a Mommy and Me group
the meeting is full of married women.

They complain about what it costs
two-parent families to pay for childcare.

Fearful they will sum me up
if I tell my story—

young, unemployed,
my son one of the 70 percent of black children
growing up in a single-parent household—

I sit with my son in my arms.

Never say a word.

Tradition

Christmas.
Crystal's parents have gathered family and friends.
Everyone floats
in and out of the kitchen
for mini mountains
of greens, mac and cheese, candied yams, and chicken.

Crystal's mother Pat
taps my hips.

"What's this? What's this?" she jokes.
I laugh.

Valley-deep glory
at how motherhood
has rounded my slim shape.

Pat is a nurse.
I am too shy to pull her aside:

I tried to breastfeed and could not.
What causes inverted nipples?
Are they common?

Why do I,
my breasts,
feel broken?

With Good Fortune

It's called *Nocturnal lagophthalmos*.

Khari's eyes are half-open as he sleeps.

When we visit
Cousin James and Cousin Vivien,
Cousin Vivien asks,

Was he born with a caul?

Down South, they called it a veil.
Those children can see and speak to ghosts.
Tell the future.

"There is no way I can know," I say.

Cousin Vivien shakes her head,
says,

And wouldn't it be just like them
to see a black child born with magic,
keep it a secret
from its half-asleep mother who is
flat on her back
and can't see what is happening past her belly?

Relactation

The soy formula is not working.
Weepy rashes.
Khari constantly scratches.

One snowstorm,
I walk two miles before I find an open store
selling the Aveeno to soothe him in his baths.

Mommy speaks to Aunt Verne
who tells Cousin Darryl,

whose ears are glued
to WBAI.

Call La Leche League.

I sit there with Khari,
like the consultant instructed,
trying to get him to suckle.

He wails.

For weeks I was like a tree leaking sap.
Sweet soak of colostrum/milk, long gone.

Khari is four months old.
He turns away from this foreign, unproductive terrain.

After an hour, my resolve
as cracked as my nipple skin,

I boil water for bottles.
Failure boils my blood.

Had I known

I would be denied
joy and peace
glossy pamphlets and posters promised,

babies looking up at their mothers,
tiny hands resting against their smiling mothers' breasts,
easily ingesting
antibodies, beta carotene,

protection

against asthma, obesity, diabetes,
and sudden infant death,

I would not have squeezed my chest and prayed
for these useless breasts when I was eight.

I fill a bottle with formula.

Let him feed.

A Confession

Tanya and our friend Sonya
take turns holding Khari,
kiss him and coo.

I am afraid they will think less of me if I tell them how hard this all is:

piles of baby clothes   my dumpy clothes   to wash and dry
sponges mops   wet spots   cooking crumbs
golden arches of urine   the stink of the Diaper Genie
Khari waking up   every two hours pacing the floor
rocking arm cramps from holding Khari for hours every day
I have no money no one to talk to   while Mommy and Daddy
are at work
Donna back at Spelman my friends working   in graduate school
traveling

This guilt I feel for complaining about any of it.

I read about a mother so tired she shook in her sleep.
I feel smaller than her,
smaller than my mother,

smaller than Great-Grandmother Lena,
who raised seven children
on a North Carolina farm with Great-Grandfather John.
Her feet seemed planted in the kitchen,
rolling pin in hand,
grandchildren gathered around the table as their parents worked,

smaller than Grandma Pauline,
who used a washboard to launder the clothes for the six of them.
Hung them on a clothesline.
She raised all five children alone in the forties and fifties.
All graduated from high school and employed,

smaller than Nana Sallie,

who had three miscarriages.
Her boss arranged for her to give birth to Daddy at New York Hospital.
Most Harlemites were born at Harlem Hospital in the 1940s.
This child is gonna live.
What would Tanya and Sonya think if they knew

how many days I hand Khari
over to Mommy
as soon as she gets home from work
so I can take a nap,

of the day Mom yelled at me,
You're not ready to be a mother!

I yelled something back,
but not too loud—
(deep down,
despite that white light in my belly,
I think she is right)

or when Khari
6 months old—
gurgling grunting reaching for me

                    I stood over his crib

SHUT UP
SHUT UP
SHUT UP

JUST SHUT UP

Affect

Khari's father says,
I have a girlfriend now.

I am hot and cold
all at once,
but my voice
is Dominique Dawes on a balance beam.

"That's nice."

I actually wanted you to be jealous.

I do not say so, but
I am,

of the time
he has to date
while I do this work.

I drop the receiver into its cradle.
Walk over to Khari's crib.

Watch him sleep.

How I wish I thought to say

That the sun and moon
daily trade places
surpasses
whatever it was
I found

in your arms.

Twenty-Five Years of Service

Daddy   is out of work

the ramp serviceman   holding the other side of the trunk

shifted   most of the weight   onto Daddy

Second on-the-job   injury   the first, Donna and I were
teenagers

some machine   snatched Daddy's   left index fingernail

right out   of its nail bed   it grew back   with an
inward curve

His back now out   no more fixing cars   on the side

Mom's paycheck   cannot cover   the rent

Eviction notice on the front door   where neighbors   can see

Daddy applies   to substitute teach

In the meantime Mommy gives Daddy   the certificates of deposit

she bought   for Donna and me   with our inheritance   from
Uncle Don

who demanded she see to it   we both graduate from college

"Don't disappoint me"   Uncle Don's suicide note   said

"No, Daddy!   I was saving that money for Khari's education."

"Quiet!" he snaps   heart and hands on the here and now

Millstone

Daddy and I load the groceries onto the conveyor belt

Our cashier is Mrs. Martinez

how-are-yous
how-is-the-family

She frowns

Trina is pregnant AGAIN!

Mutters under her breath

> Trina, 19
> unemployed
> lives with her mother
> who babysits her son when Trina
> wants to go out, be young

Daddy shakes his head

These children don't know how to use birth control

A flush of heat
as if
I am on stage under a spotlight

I keep packing

water   orange juice   apple juice   cans of tuna   spaghetti

baby food   diapers

Baba

I walk past my parents' bedroom.

Daddy is lying on their bed,
knees propped up.

Khari is sitting on Daddy's stomach.

They are holding hands.

Daddy is bouncing his legs.

Say
Say
Say

I rush to get my camera.
Quietly take a picture.

Say
Say
Say

Gurgling.

I close the door.

The Hunt

When Khari turns a year old,
I spend months of Sundays
scouring want ads
in the *New York Times*
and *New York Daily News*.

Finally.
A job interview at Strawberry.
Retail associate.
$5 an hour.

I borrow
a print blouse from Mom
to match my black pencil skirt.

With no one else available,
80-year-old Grandma babysits
while I go downtown,
lie
about how much I love
helping women pick out clothes.

When I get home Grandma
is pouring herself a cup of apple juice.

The glass bottle falls from her hands.
Crashes to the floor.

Glass shards scrape the floor as I sweep.
Grandma. It's OK. I've got it.

I do not take the job.

Who would take care of Khari while I go to work?

Plastic

Put on your oxygen mask
before helping anyone else, they say.

But Mom is very clear.
You feed your child first.

I turned away from her and rolled my eyes
the first time she said it.

I heat Khari's dinner and put it in his dish.
Arrange mine on my plate.

Set it down.
Turn around to put Khari in his highchair.

Too close to the edge of the counter,
the ceramic plate falls.

My sauteed corn, veggie burger, and fries
crash to the floor.

Before I can stop myself, I throw
the plastic bottle of ketchup against the wall.

Red blobs
slide down to the floor.

I cover my mouth and gasp.
Mom glares at me.

Khari wails.

I clean the wall,
mop the floor,

wishing I could dig a hole somewhere,

and bury this anger.

Triumph

Hands grip playpen rail

Khari pulls himself up
walks up one side of the frame
lays his body flat on top of the rim,
grips it
lowers himself to the floor.

Runs toward me.

I lift him up.
Put him back in the playpen.

Khari looks at me.

Come on, son.
What will you do when you encounter setbacks?

I return his grin
when Khari

reaches for the sky.

Clenches rim in the vise of his hands.

Climbs.

Prone, he swings his body around.

Lands safely on the floor.

PART III

THE MOTHER LEARNS AS SHE TEACHES

Dear Laura,

I thought Mommy would jump up and hug me.

Fordham University, Queens College,
Teachers College of Columbia University,
The New School for Social Research,
New York University, all accepted me.
"That's nice," she said.
It's Grandma.
Liver cancer.
Grandma cannot get out of bed.
Mom went to her house to care for her every evening after work.
Grandma tried to tell me from her hospital bed
what a wonderful granddaughter I am.
I walked out before she could finish her sentence.
I did not want her to see me cry.
Grandma died June 3, 1995.
Four weeks later, we drove down to D.C. so Aunt Joan could hug us goodbye.
So much I wanted to say. She was too drugged to speak.
I kept holding her hands, stroking her perfect oval nails.
She died in July.
Daddy spoke at her funeral.
His voice cracked a little, but he would not let himself break.
Mom thinks he cried in the shower.
Grandma and Aunt Joan would have been so proud—
my scholarship from NYU for prospective teachers of color
paid half my tuition.

Daddy finds me a sitter, our neighbor Mrs. White,
who cares for babies and toddlers in her home.
Do you have room for my grandson?
"I might be could," she said, and did.

I took the 6 train four days a week to Astor Place,
first to my part-time work-study job as an administrative assistant, then
classes.
I felt stupid sometimes.
Girl. I don't drink coffee.

They had to show me how to change the filter for the coffee machine.
My supervisor put a DO NOT WATER ME, I AM NOT THIRSTY sign
on what turned out to be a fake rubber tree so I would stop watering it.

$300 of the $360 I earned each month went to Mrs. White.
Most days I ate lunch a few blocks from school: a falafel and an orange for
$2.

Read for my classes, wrote papers while Khari played with his toys or slept.
Got mostly As, except two classes where I kept getting Bs.
All the black students in those two classes got Bs.
I asked some of the white students how they got As,
and they said they wrote down everything the professor said.
Purposeful metacommentary was how we were taught at Spelman.

Prospective teachers bound for a system
where brown and black children are predominant,
but no discourse around Afrocentrism
AAVE
Latino history and culture.

I wrote to Dr. Wade-Gayles for advice.
She said to get through my coursework, graduate, and then fight.
I rolled up my sleeves.
Typed my handwritten notes from class,
re-read them aloud before every blue book exam.
3.58 GPA.

Commencement, Washington Square Park.
It rained.
I told my family they did not have to come.
They took a picture of me before
I kissed Khari goodbye and rode the train downtown.
I had an umbrella, but my press-and-curl went back.
The purple dye from my graduation gown bled onto my white dress.
Robert DeNiro was our speaker, but I was too far back to see him.

As the business school grads danced around the fountain chanting,

We Have Jobs! We Have Jobs!
I wondered which public school would hire me,
make this Master of Arts in Social Studies Education worth
the loans, babysitting fees, and $2 lunches that left me hungry.

I went to every job fair I could until I found
a social studies position at Diana Sands Community Intermediate School 147
in the South Bronx,
a few blocks away from where I was born.

For the first day of school, I got my hair done in Goddess braids,
with little gold beads inside,
wore my best outfit from Burlington Coat Factory's discount rack–
a white blouse, brown slacks, and lace-up shoes.

I smiled at each student in my seventh-grade homeroom class–
20 boys and 12 girls–
shook their hands until I got to Brunilda who gave me that what-is-she-doing look.
I gave one class after another detention for talking when I talked,
not listening when I told them to line up for dismissal.
The day I tried to give them a Christmas party two of the boys fought,
threw pieces of the vegetable lasagna I cooked the night before around the room.
Many nights, as I cooked dinner, I called as many students' parents as I could.
A student's older brother said, "We talk so often I feel like we married."
I never called there again, even when that boy walked around the room,
a ruler to his crotch. "This is my dick, this is my dick!"

You got a raw deal, one of the teachers told me,
the day I slid down the wall in the bathroom with my head in my hands.

After I have enough money,
I moved into Grandma's one-bedroom apartment.
Kept her off-white carpet and yellow paisley sofa.
Khari and I shared her queen-sized bed.

One night he stays up past eleven laughing.
I dress us both and go to my parents' house.

I put him to sleep in my old bedroom, and I go back to my place.

I know, Laura. I know.

I just wanted to sleep.
Weekends grading, writing lessons, workshops, and conferences,
figuring out how to win my students over.

When I needed copies for my classes,
the school secretary took at least two days to make them,
so some Sundays, I rode the express bus downtown to Staples on 34th
Street.

Sometimes Khari had to come with me, and he ran around the store.
I tried holding him between my feet as I placed the papers in the machine.
I wagged my finger in Khari's grinning face, telling him to behave.
One time I popped him on his cheek.
A lady stared at me.

Khari laughed.

Shift

Donna, do you remember the first time you saw Khari?

Thanksgiving of '93,
you flew in Tuesday night and had gone straight to bed
without saying hello to any of us
because Daddy brought you home from the airport
so late after his shift
and when you arose the morning next morning
you had unraveled your twists,
every strand of that thick head of hair exploding
towards the ceiling.

I was holding Khari.

You reached for him,
cradled him in your left arm
and rocked him back and forth.
He stirred.
Opened his eyes,
looked up and I swear, he jumped at the sight
of his pretty aunt surrounded by that shock of black hair.

Oh, he's ugly!
You laughed.
I smiled at your sarcasm,
knowing from the girth of your grin he was adored.

You were nineteen.

I knew you would tell Khari,
forget that Aunt stuff, just *call me Donna*,
that he would nap against the hills of your bosom,
that he would run to your lap,
he will sit on your bed throughout his adolescence,
soaking up secrets—
how you managed to steal library books,
the cigarette you smoked in the girls' bathroom in sixth grade,
the weed you smoked twice in college but didn't like.
Donna, the day you said,

You're always leaving him over here!
You're a mother when it's convenient!

Truth's echo stung.
Barb broke off.
There was swelling.

That was why I pushed you.
Hollered when you pushed me back.

Please forgive me.

Legacy

When we were babies, Mom loved being a full-time mother. Bought pieces of felt in primary colors, cut them into portraits of cats and dogs and clowns to hang on our bedroom walls. Sewed mod dresses for herself, frilly dresses for us. Baked oatmeal cookies for my kindergarten class.

But the seventies were hard on single-income families. When I was six, and Donna, three, Mom went back to work as a secretary at MetLife. Mom, on wash days, vacuumed the floors and furniture. Piles of colors and whites in front of the washer. Other wash days, she laid a towel on the bathroom floor so I, then, Donna, could kneel over the bathtub, clean wet washcloths to protect our eyes from the shampoo. She bent over us one at a time lathering, then conditioning our thick hair, wrapping our heads in towels until our hair stopped dripping, then sectioning, combing out, blow drying our hair, braiding two cornrows in the front, then ponytails with barrettes on the ends, when she did not have the energy to press and curl our hair, then hers.

I was ten when I brought her a shirt and pants to iron just before I dressed for school, and she looked at me, and said, *Enough*. Gave me the pressing cloth. Showed me how to iron a proper crease, ushering new dawn, the how-tos of womanhood:

how to set a proper table, fold a flat sheet properly so it lies adjacent to the bed skirt, how to thread a needle, sew holes in socks and tears in shirts, where to write the return and recipient address on an envelope, how to

use home keys so well I don't have to look down when I type, how to
wrap birthday and Christmas gifts, write thank you notes, how to scrub
rufescence from our underthings before we threw them in the hamper, how
to arch my eyebrows with a brush, how to fill *Nothing* with thunder's rumble
when someone asks you what is wrong. They back off to avoid the lightning
strike.

When I was grown, I found a letter Grandma wrote to Uncle Reggie:
The girls are fine, but Paula is tired.

Before I wanted to be alone while I wash dishes,
I used to wonder why Mommy got on her hands and knees
to scrub the bathroom floors even though we had a mop.
Quiet time to reflect and pray.

I ask her how she did it all. She looks at me. Pauses.
You just have to dig deep down and find the strength.

Remember, This Too, Shall Pass—
is my trekking pole on the rough days.

Words

After Khari says mama
I write down every word
he learns
first no then yes then
please is "pease"
key
go
apple
outside
ball
bye
what's that
who's that
but
I squeal, clap my hands
when "b" bounces off his lips
"-air"
stretches like a bow
before "bear" launches
into the bullseye of my ears
"Say bear again,"
and Khari's cheeks
reach for his temples,

I fold him into a hug,
wish his
phonemes
morphemes
diphthongs
prefixes
suffixes
could be
forged from steel–
no, too hot or too cold–
from silk--
soft but slides--
Cotton!
Yes,
a nice cotton blend.
One tenth rayon, one tenth polyester
bendable
breathable
graspable
to rub their balm against my cheek

I would swaddle them in a blanket.
Seal them in a trunk.

Moniker

Hi, Khari's mother,
Khari's friends

sing-songy call out
when they see me.

I would have been told
as a child,

No, that is Mr. / Mrs. / Miss
Proper Surname,

Miss Mary or Mr. Bill,
if they were like family.

Khari's mother
as if

I have no other name,
no other identity.

What is it that Khari
tells them about me

that inspires
this glimmer-gleam in their eyes

these smiles
too sweet for admonition.

The Learning Tree

After Khari graduates from pre-school,
I find an Afrocentric school in the Bronx.

> I will not let Khari see himself,
> his people, on the margins,
> as I did as a second grader--

> *1492,*
> *Columbus sailed the ocean blue.*

> Bragging on Benjamin Franklin,
> my seven-year-old nose in the air.

> *Humph! That's nothing!*

> when Mom spoke about
> Benjamin Banneker surveying Washington D.C.

> "Don't ever put down your people!"

> I read the few African American books in our school library,
> every issue of *Ebony Jr.* that arrived in the mail,
> the books Daddy brought home.
> Muriel and Tom Feeling's *Jambo Means Hello.*
> taught me to count to ten in Swahili.

The forty minutes from home to that Afrocentric school,
three buses to get there,
no money for a car,
are rocks at the shoreline.

Like a river, I change course.

My old elementary school is down the street.
My second-grade teacher, now the school librarian,
makes sure he is in the best kindergarten class.

As unfamiliar words appear,
my fingers are chisels.
Sound it out, I sing.
Together, we glue syllable-splinters back.

When Khari demands definitions,
I tell Khari,
Look it up.
As Daddy did for me.

I buy Khari dozens of books.
I point at street signs,
billboards, buildings
and exclaim, *Read that!*

We board buses and trains for
flag football
kung fu

and music school,

inspired by Cousin Eric,
a jazz percussionist,

and to honor our ancestors,
banned from their talking drums.

Exemplar

Before I was born,
Daddy volunteered nights to guard I.S. 148,
across the street from our apartment
in Fulton Terrace.

Silver gleam of a knife appeared.
That night God and the ancestors
must have shone the light of compassion
into those hoodlums' eyes.

Had Daddy said,
I will worry about me and mine,
no one would have blamed him.

He kept believing,
I am because we are, therefore, you will be.

When Donna and I attended P.S. 160,
Daddy assisted teachers on his days off.

Everybody respected Mr. Cherry,
especially the boys
he counseled.
Daddy kept their secrets,
no matter how hard I pried.

My son in the school system,
Daddy's light as lodestar,
I spread my wings like Aset.

I command seats
on the P.T.A.,
its executive board,
School Leadership Teams,
C-30 Committees.

In My Footsteps

Donna is 23 and pregnant,
and I am thrilled,
though it wasn't part of The Plan.
I remind Donna that she has a good job,
health insurance,
our parents and family,
her friends,
and me.

Maybe it was God,
my desire for another child,
or an almost-brother or sister for Khari,
but I rail,
You can't do that
and slam down the phone
when Donna tells me she is thinking about not keeping it.

Our cousin Kiameshia,
also knows this baby is supposed to be here.
When she comes to visit,
she makes sure Donna
is the first to hold baby Nasif.

These baby boys
in her arms,
on her lap,
Donna asks me to be her Lamaze coach.

I do what the husbands/fathers do.
Coax her through the breathing.
Hold her hand.
Prop her back against my chest.

I Chose Her Middle Name

When I arrive at the hospital, Donna is sleeping.
Swollen.
Long white stockings up to her hips.

Where is my niece?

When they hand her to me,
two orbs of amber.

She's beautiful, I sob.

Donna names her Anike.
Ah-knee-kay.
God is a gracious one/he has answered the prayers/prize possession.

I announce, *her middle name is Njeri*.
　　　Kikuyu:
　　　Belongs to a warrior.

I swipe crumbs from the seams
of the foldaway bed.
I lie down but refuse to slumber.

While my sister sleeps,
I promise God I will guide her
around my maternal missteps,
lend listening ears and helping hands.

Sheath of light
from the
Waxing Crescent Moon,
I wonder

if Anike Njeri is asleep in the nursery,
her eyes,
half-open.

Oath

Monday,
I fall asleep on the sofa before I put Khari to bed. Something tells me to wake up. The echo of Khari's voice is in the hallway. When I realize he has unlocked and opened the front door by himself, I jump up, pull him back, lock the door, beat myself up over my fatigue.

Tuesday,
Before I take Khari home, his after-school program teacher pulls me aside. *He's not listening!*

Wednesday,
Leo's mother meets with me. They are homeless. I offer to bring twenty dollars so she can wash their clothes. As I fold our laundry that night, I smell hot glass/burning milk/butter.
Our macaroni and cheese! Khari hugs me. "It's OK, Mommy." As I cook turkey burgers instead, I open a package of Oreos. We pry them apart, turn them over, cream hitting our tongues first.

Thursday,
Bits of crayon beneath Khari's fingernails remain from the day before. Twenty minutes to scrub it all out. Drop him off at my parents' house so Mom can drop Khari at school before she goes to work, and I run to one of the two buses to get to 170th and Webster Ave. I am fifteen minutes late. Again. My assistant principal, hard bass in his voice, yells at me in front of my homeroom class. I sag in my chair and cover my face. My student Noemi hugs me. And I remember that I forgot to bring the money for Leo.

Most Friday afternoons I slump on the sofa once we get home. But tonight,
Ray is in town.
I am showering and getting dressed to go out. Loud banging. Frequent
ringing of my doorbell.
Peppermint mask on my face. Four policemen who ask if I am OK. They
got a call that we were being held hostage. Khari, bored, had picked up the
phone and dialed 911 as a joke.

Saturday,
I pull a muscle in my back as I walk home with the groceries.

Sunday,
Anike squalling in the background,
Donna and I say over the phone,

I will not have another child unless I get married.
This is too hard.

My Stargazer

Khari,
my superhero,

who runs through my house,
his grandparents' house,

with a cape and a mask
rescuing who-knows-who from who-knows-what,

who used his school scissors
to cut the cord to his desk lamp while it was on

while I scrubbed out the bathtub
for his nightly bath,

was too busy laughing
to be afraid of my screaming and hysteria.

His teachers tell me that Khari is a smart, nice boy
who sometimes daydreams when he should stay on task.

I nod, and promise to speak to him,
my stargazer,
who,
as I stroke his face,
sleepily holds my hand in his,
hallway light,
his shield
against mysteries of the night.

Gasp

The eczema   *You will have to watch him for asthma*

Not in my family,   or   his father's

Eight years old   nonstop coughing wheezing   ambulance

I break two nights   fold-out bed on the floor

prednisolone for a week

my ear Khari's chest   whistling   in the chamber   nebulizer

albuterol   chamber   face mask commands nose and mouth

mouthpiece   breathe deep until white spirals of mist   disappear

droning motor hum   hissing steam   May God hear me

Bible spine crackles   Genesis 9:3

Everything that lives   and moves about   will be food for you.

Just as I gave you green plants   I now give you everything

Limit dairy   avoid family pets

Woodroot tonic's   chaney roots   cleanses blood

sarsaparilla   boosts blood

African cayenne eliminates excess mucus

Khari   breathes easier   but guilt clogs my chest

am I to blame

                                   breast is best

The Bond

Like Cousin Saundra,
who walked us up and down Greenwich Village
with Eric and Kiameshia,
our small brown bodies splashing
around the fountain in Washington Square Park,
Donna and I endeavor to be like daylilies.
Make the most of our native soil.

The Museum of Natural History.
Khari and Anike gawk at the dinosaurs.
Chase each other through Central Park.
Point at and inhale flowers at the Bronx Botanical Gardens.
South Street Seaport,
we pose for pictures with Brooklyn Bridge as backdrop.
Dance Africa at BAM.
We clap to the beat of the drums and dance in our seats.

Kiameshia's house in Philadelphia.
Cousins run around the yard,
yelp and scream upstairs.
Birthday parties every year, bowling to miniature golf.
Every kid movie from *Toy Story* to *A Bug's Life*.

Wade the waters of Pear Tree Point Beach.
Roam the streets of Providence, Rhode Island.
Tourist boats of Mystic, Connecticut.
Madison Square Garden to see the Knicks.
Niagara Falls. Maid of the Mist, Cave of the Winds.

Khari and Anike hug. Giggle.
Shout *Nothing!* in unison when we ask what they are doing
when they escape our eyesight.

Summer of 2001, we mean to,
but do not take Anike and Khari to the World Trade Center.

We'll do it next year, we say.
It'll be there.

Single, Sassy, Satisfied

After the bills,
I stash a few hundred from each paycheck into Khari's college fund.
Rare to have money,
the energy,
the eight hours it will take for box braids.
I cut my nails myself,
push my cuticles back
with my thumbs in the shower,
like Mommy taught me.
My boyfriend says,
These women around here? Their hair and nails is done!
I let him chase after the gem he wanted on his arm.
Every year, several times a year,
my students ask me if I'm married.
One of my eighth graders
says I am grumpy
because I do not get enough sex.
I call his father,
who makes him apologize,
but the left side of my chest still hurts.
Alarmist articles—
educated Black women
the most unmarried group—
scare me into believing
there are not enough
available single men.
Tanya gives me
Michele McKinney Hammond's
Single, Sassy, Satisfied.
I buy Iyanla Vanzant's *In the Meantime.*
So much work to do—
parsing my love life,
reflecting on its lessons—
to convince myself
I am enough,
and deserve my soulmate.
While I wait,
can't I just be held?

Him

his
tongue in
ricochet

mouth to
mouth

When
he set

my harmony

on fire

I ran
around in
circles

like
chickens evading
the falling ax.

The Audacity of Desire

I call Mom and tell her my head hurts.
I just need a few hours.

She says she will watch Khari,
too kind to question me about why I have so many headaches.

Thirty years of marriage and motherhood,
she deserves a child-free house.

I know what she will say if I am honest
about why I want her to babysit.

Hermetically sealed for two years,
I cannot stand to be this holy.

I need a few hours to revel in his raillery.
If I utter this truth, if my family

meets him,
they see his eyes,

they will tell me not to be like dust,
dust settles.

Like dust, one day
I will be swept away,

but tonight
my back in slow arch towards the floor

breath caressing bosom,
D'Angelo stoking strokes,

circles and poles
until I quiver in As and Os.

Reunion

Two years since his father has seen him.
Khari is five.

D.C. for our family reunion.
His father living nearby,
I invite him to our hotel.
He comes.

Starshine in Khari's eyes.
As father and son talk,
I wear a paper mâché smile,
even after Khari says,

Sometimes I don't behave but when I am with my father,
I am just regular.

I say nothing.
Feed your child first.

We three hang out in the pool.
His father launches his body into the bottom.
Khari watches him while I cling to the wall.

His father swims over to me,
runs his fingers along the back of my legs and my toes.
Those nights in his grandmother's basement.
I do not push him away.

He records Khari
doing a goofy dance,
then me,
posing and rapping.

We laugh.
Khari says,
This is the best day of my life!

A Bit of Truth

How come you're not with my father?

I pause.

I never lie to Khari,
but I spare my six-year-old
the monster his father inhales,
the why,

the time
his father missed the second half of a weekend visit
because he had sold the camera
he borrowed from a friend
to record footage of Khari
for our trip to Central Park.
"I don't want Khari to see me like this."

I only reply, "We don't get along."

Khari rolls his toy car along the rim of the dresser and says,

He ought to be here with his son instead of having fun

somewhere else.

Restraint

You have no idea of the sacrifices I have had to make.

"Tell me about them. I want to know,"
Khari's father says.

I shake my head.
Too much to sum up.

I want to slap him hard enough
to make him bite his tongue.
Then smile.

And say,

See?
Blood
tastes just like postpartum tears.

Compassion

I am wondering, with all the labor required
of a working single mother,
what will Khari remember of me
beyond travail,
when
my eight-year-old,
sneakers squeaking against the floor
of our new two-bedroom apartment,
tugs my shirt,
pulls my dishwater-wet hands,
and leads me towards the TV.

"Mommy, look!"

Black and brown children
crying
thin
too hungry
too sick
to wave away flies sitting on their eyes.
Their mothers rock them helplessly.

"Mom, can we send them money?"

I smile at Khari and the expanse of his heart.

I write a check to Feed the Children.
Sign up as a sponsor for Childreach.

With money and bimonthly letters
we extend our hands across the Atlantic Ocean,

to a boy named Da Sie in Burkina Faso.

Model of a Man

When Khari is nine, we go to Boston to visit Terrence,
my best friend from Morehouse. Khari's godfather.

Met first week of freshman year,
on the line for a roller coaster at Six Flags during AUC Day.

Forty-five minutes in August Georgia sun.
Which school do you attend? Where are you from?

An English major from Fort Wayne, Indiana.
A Christian. Intelligent. Handsome. Looked like D-Nice.

Friendly, funny, and a little shy.
He kept a picture of his family on his dresser.

See, we're having intellectual discussions, we said,
on the nights when our peers were hitting the clubs.

He, like our other male friends, always
walked us back to Spelman to make sure we were OK.

Daddy and Mommy loved him.
How is Terrence, Mommy always asked, and laughed.

After graduation, he wrote for the *Cleveland Plain Dealer*.
M. Div. from Harvard, earning his Ph.D. at Brown.

We tour Harvard Square.
Laugh as we imitate open back rounded vowels, nasal consonants,

and a sweatshirt hanging in a store window.
I paah-ked my caaahhh in Haah-vadddYahhhdddd.

We walk around Providence.
Sit on a bench atop a hill for Khari's funny stories.

Terrence drives us to Newport.
We tour gilded mansions.
I stand by the balcony doors.
Waves breaking rocks.

At the beach,
as I sit on the sand,

Terrence bounces a soccer ball off his right knee,
then left, kicks it to Khari, who returns the shot.

Terrence lifts Khari in the air.
I take a picture.

Terrence spins Khari in a circle.
I laugh at Khari's giggle.

I let the Atlantic hit my legs.
Rejoice in its salty perfume.

Wellness

With Donna's and Mom's help, I whittle space for me.

I join a gym. Several nights after work, we fluffy women dance our way into salty sweat. Weights burn my biceps into half-moons. After a few months, I stop going. I cannot keep up with cooking, cleaning, PTA meetings, lesson planning, and grading.

When we visit the Jersey malls, my friend Iveliz laughs at me as I run to the dressing room of NY & Company, arms filled with blouses, pants, and skirts that become six bags in the trunk of her car, as if I will never shop again.

The occasional class at Frederick Douglass Creative Arts Center. Poetry. Creative Non-Fiction. The Short Story. A classmate tells me she hears *violins* in one piece. I rip it up.

Got little more than a two-step, but I love to dance. S.O.B.'s is my spot when Raynard comes up from Miami, and then it's The Shadow when Patrick visits from Atlanta.

One summer night in a short purple floral dress, long box braids, my arms beating air like a ceiling fan to the backbeat—Mobb Deep's *Quiet Storm*, DJ Kool's *Let Me Clear My Throat*—
a man swings me around, drops to his knees, and admires my legs. Zakeha has lost me in the crowd, and has the DJ call my name when she is ready to go.

Driver ogles me from the rearview. Steering wheel in his left hand, he reaches for my legs with his right, as I smack his grasp away, demand he keep his eyes on the road, as I pray for safe return to my parents' house

and sleeping son.

Trained Up

November 23, 2003/age nine/dressed in black/Khari faces the
congregation/as the choir sings/
Take Me To The Water/he is led to the baptism pool/as I/thirteen years
before/arms folded across his chest/Khari holds his breath/as he is dipped
backwards/and brought back up, anew

as I watch/crying from my pew in the balcony/overjoyed that Khari/though
I never got him to Sunday school/we missed more Sunday services than we
made/was listening/to the sermons he was present for/grace at the dinner
table/our nightly prayers.

As Khari is led out of the baptismal pool, the congregation applauds,

I remember the day

Reverend Butts announced/*The doors to the church are open*/I walked down to
the pulpit/
shook his hand/before the deacons led me to the Blue Room/to walk me
through my initiation/the Bible classes/what to wear on my baptism day/
receiving the Right Hand of Fellowship

I was eighteen/missing what my Christian college friends who grew up in
the church seemed to have/inner peace/self-confidence/sense of purpose/
what I had when I sat cross-legged, book of Bible stories in my lap/what I
slowly lost/us churching mostly on Christmas or Easter/
Daddy working/bone-tired many Sundays/*Man can make his own heaven and*

hell right here/
he said/when I was a teen/when he/like me/wondered why the rich
prospered while the poor/the meek/wondered after/waited on the day they
would inherit the Earth

but he, like me/had a mustard seed of faith in his chest/planted by Nana and
Pop-Pop,
whose father John/was a Primitive Baptist/Hassell, North Carolina/a slim
man/straw hat/straw hanging from his mouth/who walked in front of his
charging bull/as it went for Aunt Ann and her red polka dot dress/he did
not blink as he commanded/*Get back in that pen*/bull retreated/
he tipped his hat/told Aunt Ann to go back in the house and change her
dress.

Pop-Pop and Daddy in suits, Nana and Aunt Joan in Sunday dresses/Daddy
sang in the choir at St. Luke's Episcopalian/off West 141st and Convent/
later joined Abyssinian/until the Air Force and worldly demands pulled
Daddy away.

The morning of my baptism/I brushed my hair back to fit under the
baptismal scarf/knelt on my knees/*God, please come into my life*/a bolt of
energy flowed head to toe/I shuddered/put my hand over my heart

Bounce

I.

My boyfriend and I blast "La Di Dadi" in the living room.

My parents hear Slick Rick say *bitch*.

The *look*.

Fourteen, we freeze.

I leap to press stop on the tape deck,

glad they are never home

when I scream-sing along with "Darling Nikki."

II.

A friend at Morehouse plays "Just Don't Bite It."

No one else in the room is mad but me

at the voiceover, a man whose *bitch*

misunderstood fellatio until he gave her

N.W.A.'s book about the art of doing it right.

I start listening to what I wop to.

III.

June 5, 1993.

Reverend Butts' rally against negative rap lyrics.

Daddy and I applaud the speakers.

Kool Moe Dee's sister is one of them.

Piles of cassettes and CDs in the middle of Adam Clayton Powell Jr.

Boulevard.

Steamroller never turned on.

Counter-protestors.

Daddy and I argue with one, a woman around my age

who wants to flatten our concerns.

Lectures us on long history of urban lit,

merits of Iceberg Slim.

This is about what our children are listening to,

Daddy shoots back.

IV.

Khari's fourth grade trip to Philadelphia.
He is beside me on the bus, happy his mom is here.
Girls sit with girls, boys sit with boys,
chatting and giggling,
some with CD players, headphones,
mouthing words, bopping heads.
Khari's friend asks if he wants to hear 50 Cent's album.
Khari looks at his friend. Then at me.

Because Khari looked at me,
did not answer his friend,
I know Khari will not call a woman
out of her name in my presence,
will likely not be the kind of man
to aim for a high body count,
but he is too young for The Candy Shop.

No, I am sorry. He cannot.

His friend nods, goes back to his seat.
Khari's neck is slightly red.

As Khari, his classmates scurry, squeal
around the Ben Franklin Museum,
pose for pictures next to the crack of the Liberty Bell,
I think about how easily bitch/ho/thot
glides my students' tongues.

I vow to have conversations about the content
of music and movies when Khari is a teen,
and to listen as much as I talk.

For Posterity

Grudges grow
from rage
swallowed whole.
Look to bees.
They sting,
then die.

Grace

Graduation from fourth grade.

Daddy looks at me.
Puts his hand on my shoulder,
leans over to whisper in my ear:

Take a picture with Khari and his father.

I exhale an updraft of anger,
slacken tightened lips.

Feed your child first.

I walk over to Khari's father
who is standing next to Khari and grinning,
as if he had been there for bedtime stories,
homework sessions,
to iron his school uniforms,
hours of school meetings,
trips to the library,
and paid for the dozens of books
from Scholastic book fairs
and Barnes and Noble.

I lift my voice by two octaves.
"Let's take a picture together."

Daddy smiles
as Khari eases himself between his parents,
holds his award for reading twenty-five books
beneath his heart.
Cheese!

His teacher offers to photograph all of us.
We seven,
a ring of love.

A Death of Innocence

Ten-year-old Black boy
who loves to joke and laugh,
has a thirty-two-year-old mother,

is found on the sofa
with the memoir

of a thirty-two-year-old mother,
her husband accused, hung,
for raping a white woman,
whose fourteen-year-old son
loved to joke and laugh,
wore his father's ring,
visited,
A Good Place to Raise A Boy,

did/did not whistle
near/at a white woman

his Uncle Mose,
shotgun in the back,
unsure of how many were out there
in the middle of Mississippi night
how far they would go
how many of his family,
neighbors, he would lose,
begged them
not to take the boy

Well,
if you know any of us tomorrow,
you won't live to be 65

his Aunt Lizzie, pleading,
offering money,

Get back in that bed.
I want to hear the springs squeak.

This ten-year-old boy is shocked,
that no one came running
towards the screams in the plantation shed

bones breaking,
his teeth,
the prettiest things
his mother had ever seen in her life, knocked
out until there were only two

gin fan, barbed wire piercing skin
like cotton bolls
beneath neutral witness of
blazing Southern sun

how his mother
smelled his body at the funeral parlor
from two blocks away

she saw
his light hazel brown eyeball
resting on his right cheek,
daylight
through the hole in his head.

Let the world see what I've seen.

Her Bo gone,
she considered ending it all
right before a reporter called to inquire about
what she would do next with her life.

Return to school to become a teacher,
she said,
ashamed to admit she contemplated
which window to jump out of,
to avoid landing on the playing children below.
She worried the flare of her white dress would
reveal her underthings as she'd fall.

The mother of the ten-year-old Black boy
almost retrieves the book
but his hands are clasped around it,
bronze eyes so set on the page.

PART IV

STAND

Three-Legged Chair

Dad falls and cannot get up.
His cries on the exam table, wild-river rush down the hall.

Plasmacytoma is the first diagnosis.

The last time he gives us a ride to Khari's music lesson,
Daddy looks at me.
You're going to have to learn how to drive.

Ten weeks of lessons
at Colwell's driving school.

"Come on, Ms. Cherry, let's go!"
My road test examiner snaps, as she taps on my dashboard.

I paused too long at a stop sign,
but I pass.

Plasmacytoma morphs into multiple myeloma.
Because it will not do much, he refuses chemotherapy.

Instead, he goes to Harlem Hospital
for blood transfusions.

Osteolytic lesions make holes in his bones.
Daddy shrinks five inches from 6'3.

Takes half an hour to walk 3 blocks.
Then wheelchair bound.

Donna and I de-ice his car when it snows.
Do his laundry.

I need you to move my car.
A baby blue 1992 Dodge Grand Caravan.

I line up besides the car ahead,
reverse 45 degrees
but ten times, I am too far from the curb.

I sweat.
Swear.
Stop.
Close my eyes…

Admitted Students Weekend at Spelman.
I fly to Atlanta without Daddy because he has to work.
Seventeen, alone in a hotel room, I call home,
terrified by cricket-quiet Georgia night.

"Daddy, when are you going to get here?"

Tomorrow. Carla, I need you to do this for me.

"OK, Daddy."
I stop sniffling and watch TV.

The Sunday before my road test.
Donna and I crack jokes as I drive
Daddy's Buick Skylark along Mosholu Parkway.

When I approach the Saw Mill Parkway,
Daddy says, "Turn right."
My first time driving on a highway.

Daddy no!
"Do it," he said.

My hands lock around the steering wheel.
Forward lean at the waist at the sight of the Hudson.
Almost in tears across the Tappan Zee Bridge.
He wouldn't let me stop until we reached Nyack.
As Donna drives back to the Bronx, I look over at Daddy.
Proud.

I need you to do this for me.

Turn on the ignition.
Forward.
45 degrees to the left.
Reverse.
Straighten the wheel.

Six inches from the curb.

Accolade

I prop his pillows
so Daddy can sit
up in bed
while he eats

As I hand him
his plate--

flounder with
pineapple garnish
on a bed of spinach--

Daddy looks at me.
Says,
You're my hero

That smile
North Star
glint
in his eyes

has nothing
to do
with the food

Oh
to be so
absolved

admired

Gallant Soldier

Daddy tells his doctors he wants to come live with me.
He cannot walk up and down the stairs at home.

I give Khari's bedroom to Daddy, and Khari lives with Mom.
His home health aide is lazy and always late.
Mommy comes over to care for Daddy while I work,
cares for Khari and Anike after school until Donna and I get home.
I cook his meals, give him the dozen vitamins he insists on taking,
do his laundry, empty his urinal, attend School Leadership Team
meetings at work and Khari's school,
drive Khari and Anike to their music lessons.

Motherhood and caretaking are two sides of a coin,
but given to one person, oil, and water.
An awful mix.

All of us need some joy.

For the first time, I buy a Christmas tree for my house
so the six of us can celebrate together.
Donna and I buy and wrap up toys and clothes for the kids.
As everyone sleeps, I clean the kitchen for a nice breakfast.
Christmas morning, we grown-ups smile
as wrapping paper flies in the air and floats to the floor.

Daddy's nurse, Diane,
tells me that I cannot care for him at my house any longer.

He needs a proper hospital bed,
pain meds,
and I
don't need all that stress and worriation.
I tell her that I want him to stay.

Mr. Cherry, even iron wears out.

I run to my parents' house,
collapse in tears
on the left side of the bed where Daddy used to sleep.

I call out to God—
Please help me.

As Daddy sleeps at the hospital, one of the deacons visits.
Tears run down his face.
He calls Daddy a gallant soldier.

May 16, 2005.
Daddy, deep in morphine-sleep.
I hold his hand.
My phone rings, and it is Cousin Vivian.

Are you ready?

The Interview
December 2004

Daddy never admits to his daughters
that he will die.

He leaned on his cane and told his nurse,
I plan to see my granddaughter graduate from high school.
Anike was four.

Daddy and I are home alone.
He sits in my black leather chair,
its tall back supporting his weakening spine.

Many family photos of him,
but I have nothing to record his voice and laughter.

I want to capture every bit of his essence.
Christmas is an easy place to begin.

"How did Nana and Pop-Pop celebrate Christmas?"

My parents would buy a tree and decorate it. We used to leave stuff out for Santa to eat. We would write letters to Santa Clause about what we wanted for Christmas, and Santa would always answer the note in my father's handwriting. When I was a child I got presents. Clothes. Toys. The best toy I got was an electric train. When I started earning more money I bought the grass and accessories for it.

My father was a better father than I was. He appreciated his children more.

He would do more Christmas stuff.

I would get the presents, but your mother did all that other stuff.

I was too tired.

To hear my father, who,

always had a side hustle, look to his father,

who worked two jobs and always had a side hustle,

whose favorite hymn was

May The Work That I've Done Speak for Me,
and say,

My father was a better father than I was,

reminds me of how I am sapling

next to my mother's redwood trunk.

Khari clings to me. Says he loves me.

Maybe I am a better mother than I think.

Thank you, God.

Thank you, Daddy,

for wells of wisdom to drink from.

Heartburn

Now that Daddy is gone, I understand
why my mother
sometimes
rocks in place in our pew,
does not answer
when I ask what is wrong
as her tears have their way.

The million words in English
all stagger,
wobble,
under this boulder of grief.

When I cannot sleep,
I seek solace in serotonin highs.

Spoon after spoon of butter pecan ice cream.
One chocolate chip cookie,
one potato chip
after another,
until the box or bag is fully deprived.

Gastric acid overwhelms sphincter.

I cough hard enough to gag.
Spew chyme and bile.

Acid stalks nose and throat.
Floats on breath.
Voice, a light rasp, horrifies.
Sounds like someone is choking me.

Acid reflux disease.
The doctor *could* prescribe antacids,
but gives me an alkaline diet to follow.

I do not know how to make time for therapy
with an eleven-year-old to raise,
dozens of students to teach.

I pray.

"God. Thank you for the blessings of faith, family, love, food, and shelter.
I am coming to you because I have leaned so hard
on my parents for guidance along this motherhood journey.
Sometimes my hold on it feels thin as thread."

Ever look at a spider web?
Daughter, spider silk is stronger than steel.
You have everything you need.
In your times of trials and tribulations,
lean on Me.

First step, self-care.
I stop binge eating.
Drink nothing but tall glasses of water.

One day, I am cleaning my bookshelves.
I find Cousin Alice's book of poetry,
Up Close and Personal
that she gave me at Daddy's wake.

OK, Daddy. I hear you.

I read it.
Parse my poetry notebook.

Ink leans into cursive.
Like water,
poems extinguish flames.

Threadbare

Khari at eleven, hands me the book I bought him about boys and their bodies.

Do you have any questions?

"How did you meet my dad?"

We met at an open mic. We read our poems to each other.
Went on nice dates. We used to talk a lot and laugh.

"So what happened?"

We just went on our separate ways.
I have no regrets about having you, Khari.
You are the best part of my life.
It is fine to date, but sex is serious.
Don't do what I did.
Wait until you get married to have children.

Khari nods, says, "I know," but has a faraway look.
Every child wants their origins,
evidence they were conceived from love.

How I wish Khari had a wedding album of his parents to flip through,
cuddles in the fortress of our laps,
memories of us
at the table paying bills,
me lying across his father's chest tweezing his beard,
his father dedicating a love song to me on the radio.

This threadbare story.
Pithy admonitions.
I have come up short.

After Khari is in bed, I go for a walk.
Sit on a bench and watch the night sky.

Daddy, are you watching over us?
A quasar pulses.

PART V

JEJUNITY

Psalm 5 for Black Boys

But let all black boys take refuge in You.

Let
the confounding black boys
the nerdy black boys
bookish black boys
playful black boys
boisterous black boys
shy and quiet black boys
athletic black boys
tech-savvy black boys
empathetic black boys
the righteous black boys
the spiritual black boys
the rebellious black boys
the searching black boys
poetic black boys
truth-telling black boys
prophetic black boys

sing and shout,
rejoice in you.

Surely, LORD, you will
bless them and keep them.

Surround them with your favor,
armor
and shield.

A Dare

Imagine a boy
and his friends after school.
They go to the deli across the street.

Take something! I dare you!

He steals a bottle of lemonade.

The owner catches him.
He is placed in the back of the security car.
His classmates watch and laugh.

His mother gets home from a long day.
Her answering machine is flashing.
She listens to the message.
Hears "Neighborhood Police" and grabs her keys.
She runs to the bus.
Asks the driver if he can go any faster.

Her son is sitting in a chair.
His eyes are red, plush with tears.

She nods as the officer tells the story.
She yesses him until he says they can go.
She announces with confidence:

You will never see him again.

Walking the half mile home,
she considers unbuckling her leather belt.
Wrapping it around her hand.
Striking her son about his head, his back.

She beats him thusly:

Your grandfather would be so ashamed.

"Oh my God," her son cries,
as he runs home ahead of her.

He is twelve.

Knowing how the age of black boys
is overestimated,
how they are deprived
of childhood innocence,
second chances,

they have the talk after dinner.

She reminds him
he was raised better than to steal,
that though he will not receive all he wants,
he has everything he needs,
that he must think before he acts,
that prisons are full of black men,
that if he enters the penal system,
she cannot be there to protect him.

For the first time in years,
he sleeps in her bed,
curled up next to her.

He dreams metal bars
and slamming doors.

He Asked Me To Write This Poem

When Khari is twelve, I teach him
light spritzes of Pledge   smooth swipes of the dust cloth
to vacuum floors in straight strokes   sift whites   colors and darks
fold towels in neat vertical thirds
encase mattress with fitted sheet   snap and shake flat sheet
let it cascade   pull it tight across the bed   fold ends into
triangles tuck them in

I never check that work

But foodie that I be,
sound of stainless knife cracking cutting board
draws me to the kitchen.

Khari
chopping lettuce and tomatoes
taco shells spread across the cookie sheet,
ground turkey sizzling in the pan.

I flip it with the spatula.
Pull the oregano from the cabinet.
Sprinkle.

Khari steps by my side.
Mom, you don't have to do that.

I reach for the basil.

No, Mom, really. I've got this.

I twist open its cover.

Mom, STOP!

I look up at the crinkle over his brow.
I pass him the spatula.
Raise my hands in surrender.

Venom

I'm the oddball!

Sometimes
a mother's

You're Wonderful The Way You Are

does not douse
the bonfires bullies build.

Why can't a black boy,
any boy

just be

thin,
prefer watching sports to playing,
love making friends more than fighting,
shy with girls.

If only this
black boy
had an older brother,

the kind who would teach him
to grow flowers,
practice care for the seeds he plants,

assure him
he is already enough,

it is good and right to be a virgin
until he is ready
for the responsibilities and joys,

an older brother
different from those
of some men I have known,
who were
as young as nine,
taken
to be pleasured
in the bedroom
of an older girl or woman,
slapped on the back,

proclaimed a man.

In His Hands

The day Khari graduated from middle school,
he insisted—
no more clip-on ties.

I did not know what to do
with the wide and narrow sides
of Daddy's navy-blue paisley tie.
We walked over to Mommy's for her able hands.

Before his first day of high school,
Khari found a how-to-tie-a-tie video on YouTube.

It took Khari the longest to lace his shoes at four,
but at thirteen,
in front of the mirror,
he wraps the tie evenly around his neck,
folds it into full Windsor.

He's a Poet

Mom taught me
long before I
when she brought home
real name and address
Throughout high school
Donna and I

about mentor texts
became a teacher
a copy of a resume and cover letter
cut off with pinking shears.
and college,
mimicked the objective

listed companies, job titles
infused active verbs
stated our qualifications
on the page,

in chronological order
into our duties
confidently and enthusiastically
in person.

When I heard Khari at 13

drop this piece:

Bush is a donkey
In the presidential seat
He's got the symbols of democracy
Resting at his feet

I send him to Urban Word.
Beau Sia.
Amiri Baraka.
Baba Israel.

He studies with poetic masters:

At the showcase,   we sit at the front,
pump fists   record
rap along   with Khari
commanding the stage   left to right
black fitted cap backward smiling
mic in his right hand   waving his left
calling for   lyricism in hip hop music

I'm King KC
Straight from the Boogie Down
Where we get down
Down with the movement
True artists taking back music

My voice above the applause   *That's my son!*

Fisticuffs

I.
My marrow burns.

Khari, 13,
lying on the sofa with
an ice pack near his left eye.

I demand,
What happened?

Khari had gone to the mall with a friend after school.
Three boys confronted him, unprovoked, and hit Khari in the face.
His friend, who studies martial arts, was too afraid to jump in.

II.
At age ten, I was a latchkey kid,
house keys looped around my neck.

We weren't scared most of the time.
We knew our neighbors--
best friends across the courtyard.
The Addisons, five doors down.
The Barclays, 20 feet east.
Aunt Verne's building a 50-foot walk.

Summers, we kids ran in and out of our townhouses,
screen doors slamming behind us a dozen times a day.
Front door unlocked,
bikes, roller skates, and skateboards,
double-dutch and hopscotch,
danced and rapped to the radio all day.
You listened when the grown-ups said something to you

if your mouth or behind got out of line.

I fought twice:
in pre-school I hit a fresh boy named Curtis
and he threw a rock that left a welt on my head.

Another at ten when a girl got in my face.

Daddy hung back as I did the black-girl-windmill—
arms swinging 360 degrees.
Rolling jabs.
Assured I could hold my own, Daddy broke it up.

III.
When Khari was eight, I put him in kung fu.
He liked the drills, punching the board in half,
but sparring bouts ended in frustration and tears.
His gi was stored in a drawer.

His father down South,
godfathers busy with their lives,
no one
to show him how to bend and ball up his fingers,
hold his thumbs so his hands don't get hurt,
how to bob and weave around other kids' fists
and land quick blows,

I tell Khari,
if somebody bothers you in school,
yell *Leave Me Alone,*
and pray that is all he will ever have to do.

I do not know my neighbors beyond hello,
good night,
quick how-are-yous.
I do not hand him the house keys at 13.
I am sure he will be safe
with Mom and Anike
until I pick him up.

IV.
Did you call the police, I demand.
Khari shakes his head.

Let's go file a report!
Khari says no,
surrendering to the code of the streets.

I imagine myself driving with Khari around the mall,
pointing at loitering teens:

Was it them?

like I'm going to run over other mothers' sons,
wash away blood and bone
from the chassis of my car.

Khari's bruised eye,
nubilous aura surrounding bruised ego,
feel like my fault
for not knowing how to teach him to fight,
for not saying,

Pick up a brick and go upside their heads!

I try to be
daffadowndilly gentle with myself
when I err
but times like this
I am
pumice hard.

Rise

Dear Laura,

Sis, Khari was tall enough to meet my eyes
when he started high school.

First job, at Van Cortlandt Park.
Turning soil.
Pulling weeds.
Gathering fallen limbs from trees.
He sets aside money
for his school uniforms and books,
the rest he spends as he likes.

Khari is still a little shy, but
by tenth grade,
lots of friends.
Parties
Crushes
Poetry Club
Dramatic monologue club
NY Knicks Poetry Slam.

Khari wants to be a rapper.
You should have heard his freestyle to
When They Reminisce Over You.

I love his talent,
but not
the ample drugs,
and sex
in the music industry,
the odds of Khari
earning the millions he dreams about,
and buying me a house.

I ask Khari which college he would like to attend.
He shrugs.

Because I have saved,
because Daddy,
his paternal grandmother left him money,
I do not dig deeper,
ask Khari if he *wants* to go.

Laura, what plans did you have for your children?
Did they depart from yours?

If so, what did you do?

I
read three books on getting into college.
Hours in front of my computer screen until my eyes tear:
admission requirements
acceptance and freshman retention rates
racial demographics
curricular offerings
tuition costs
college reviews.

I dream of Khari at Howard or Morehouse—
blackness at the center of his academics
but also want Khari to graduate from college
without student loans.

I only have enough money for a state school.

During our fourteen college tours
across New York, New Jersey, and Connecticut,
Khari seems excited about living on campus.

He is accepted to seven of twelve colleges.
I squeal when he chooses
a state school
known for the arts,
swipes rap dreams to the side.

At The Wheel

Learner's permit!

We are on our way to the store.
You can drive.
"Alright! Thanks, Mom."

I show him how to adjust rearview and side mirrors.
Look for blind spots.

"OK, I've got it."

Turn right, I say, at the first corner.
Khari turns the wheel,
almost kissing the curb
and a parked SUV.

Veer to the left!
Khari gets closer and closer
to the SUV's rear bumper.
No!
No!
No!
Stop!

Khari hits the brake, just shy of a direct hit.

I put the car in park.
Too shaky to talk Khari through the angles of turns,
I drive the rest of the way.

Khari says, "That's cool,"
when I promise to sign him up for driving school.

That shame does not live in needing help,
does nothing to soothe
the nib of failure in my bones
as Khari stares silently out the window.

For Naught

One day as I rode with her to work,
Daddy's friend, single mother herself,
asked why I never sued for child support.
Khari was four at the time.

Don't be stupid,
when I declared
I did not want the government's hand
in my personal affairs.

When Khari is 17,
college around the corner, and I vent
about the rent, food, tuition, cable, telephone,
car insurance, clothes, credit cards
I am juggling on my own,
my boyfriend,
father of four himself, says,
Take his father to court.

When Khari's father tells the judge
he wants a paternity test,
my knees almost buckle.

Tremors thrall my arms and legs
as Khari shakes his head at the news
that he must speak with an attorney.

Donna says,
His father felt like an animal backed into a corner.
He lashed out.

I wait outside while Khari and the lawyer review
every letter Khari's father sent us, printouts
of every Facebook post and message between them.

At my next court appearance, the judge, enraged, rules
he must pay $800 per month in support.
We never get a dime of what was overdue.

Promenade

Khari's clothes pressed sharp as his Caesar fade.
White dress shirt. Pale yellow vest.
White carnation for the jacket lapel of his black suit.

Khari's date, in a rose-colored sleeveless gown.
We parents reminisce sandbox days.
Dozens of pictures until the white stretch limo pulls up.

We greet the driver.
Take care of our children, we say with our eyes.
They stay out all night.
IHOP for breakfast.

At graduation,
Mom, Donna, Aunt Verne, Anike, Terrence, and I
defy the request not to cheer as the graduates cross the stage.
I dry my eyes before we pose for pictures.

Khari interns at an advertising firm that summer.
Wins two scholarships.

When we drop Khari off at college,
I let Donna, Anike, and Mom hug him first.

In tears, I tell Khari to go to all his classes and study hard.
Make good choices, Donna says.

Before I fall asleep that night,
I remember
sitting cross-legged in front of Nozibele,
thorny bush of fear in my chest.

You have a high possibility of success.
It depends upon the work that you do.

I stroke my linea nigra.

Tender

I cry off and on for three days.

Watch *Toy Story 3*

bawl when Andy
gives his toys to Bonnie
before I laugh
at myself,

rifle through my purse
for Tammy's number,

the pretty social work intern
on our campus
who told me she does hair
when I admired her curly fro.

I make an appointment.

If I'd Had a Daughter

That dress is too short, I say.

It's fine,
the snap in Donna's voice declaring—
she's *my* daughter.

Black baby doll dress
barely covers
Anike's seventeen-year-old hips.

After crowds gather to tell Anike
how beautifully she sang—
as I knew they would—

two elders murmur behind me
about the length of that baby doll dress.

Donna shrugs them off.
Busybodies!

But I remembered Nana
who refused to accept rides
from white men driving taxis

because.

What terrors had she,
other Black women
born before,
during,
the first half
of the twentieth century,
heard, or seen, or lived

in those days
when their best protections
were their reputations,
clothing that concealed?

Leave something to the imagination,

Mommy,
all our mothers advised,
and most of us did,

but tops/jeans/shorts
could do so much to camouflage
curves
dissuade the men on corners from
leering,
commanding
smiles

names
phone numbers,

using
crowded subway seats,
short stops,
as excuses
to fall into our flesh.

I have been worried since Anike was twelve,
the day we
walked around Chelsea,
Anike, in front, smiling back at us,

man older than me,
greasy-grinning at her—

Is that for me?

"No sir! Nuh-uh!"
I sizzle, before I tell Donna what happened.

Fourth wave feminism

demands we educators think about
how many times
we gave girls
sweatshirts,
sweatpants to wear,
called their parents to pick them up because of
short shorts
halter tops and navels,
breasts threatening to pop out of tight shirts.

So many of the boys
hung their pants low.

They heard nothing about
respect, shaming, and consent.

Anike just wanted to sing,
be her pretty self.

How woke would I be,
if I had birthed a daughter.

PART VI

THE EMERGING MAN

Metamorphosis

Chrysalis-casing cracked,
young adult leaps from flower to flower.

Monthly phone calls,
trips home now and then,
his comings and goings
are nectar—

Friends, parties, classes,
unlearning heteropatriarchy.
On-campus apartment.
Negotiating dishwashing,
floor sweeping, laundry, brotherhood.
Weightlifting.
Camping trips.
Jaunt to Virginia Beach with the fellas.
Part-time jobs on campus.
Songs he loves.

Mom, check out J. Cole's Crooked Smile.
Those lyrics!

Stand-up comedy class at Caroline's.
Twenty of us pack the joint for Khari's debut.
He overhears someone say,
That kid is going places.

When I consider a second master's—
adolescent literacy studies at Lehman College,
Khari says,
Do you.
Go for it, Mom.
This is your time.

I flutter.
Sip.
Nourished by opulent love, I soar.

Slow Bomb

I almost faint.

Fear that led to me to supervise every visit has come to fruition.

Khari's father's best friend tells me Khari's father was killed.

So much talent for writing. Technology. 43 years old.

I am sad for his wife, youngest son, and daughter,

and most of all, for Khari, who is only 19.

The request for a DNA test shook solid ground,

ruptured a fissure never to be crossed or mended.

Donna and Cousin Brian at my side,

I race along the Hutchinson River Parkway.

> Linger on the gun pointed at Khari's father's head.
> Whether he held up his wedding ring.
> Begged to see his children again.
> Did he have a chance to pray?

We knock on Khari's apartment door.

Invite him for a walk.

"I just wanted to let you know that your father is dead.

I am so sorry."

We surround Khari in a hug.

Ask if he is alright.

Yes, I'm OK.

Says no when I ask if he wants to come home.

I tell him to use his school's counseling services if he must.

Khari says he will.

I find out three years later,

Khari sought counseling,

did not feel it helped,

had days when,

no matter how hard his roommates shook him,

he could not get out of bed,

that he told his girlfriend he was afraid

that his father's fate might become his own.

A Different Beast

The echo of gunfire
since I was a child.

An NYPD firing range
a few miles north and east.

Ramarley Graham lived
twenty minutes to our west.

Because
I cannot wish away a world where
most white mothers never worry
if their sons will be chased home by cops,
shot in front of their little brothers or grandmothers,
who are threatened to be shot too,
as the system fails to prosecute,

because
abiding laws,
a loving family
and manners
will not suffice if you have Black skin,

I bring Khari to a forum facilitated
by Black law enforcement officers:

"What do you do if you are stopped by the police?"

so he will know what to do
if he is stopped and frisked.

You have the right to remain silent,
You do not have to consent to a search,
but if they suspect a weapon they can search you anyway,
Stay calm,
Keep your hands where the police can see them,
Don't run, resist, or obstruct the officers in their duties,
Do not lie or give false documents,

should not be litany
for Black boys and men.

I pray Khari has it memorized
every time he leaves the house.

Manhood in the Age of Trayvon

Another protest for Trayvon.
I go this time.

So does Khari.

There is a picture of him
on his college's website,
fire in his eyes,
firm set of his mouth,
marching with his black student union.

My son,
if / when
you must wield

the double ax
of Shango

I will not
block your way.

Archetype

Dear Laura,

Have you heard of Dr. Umar Johnson,
who says
pathology in black community
can be traced to The Average (Single) Black Mother,
who is raising her daughters to believe
black men are nothing,
raising her sons
to be the type of men she ironically
wouldn't want to date herself,
that straight black boys,
are turning gay,
psychologically castrated by their mothers.

You ain't gonna be nothin,' just like your daddy.
I should have never had you.

Sis, these pseudo-Pan-Africanists that I know
send me links to YouTube videos of Shahrazad Ali.

I,
Average Black Single Mother,
refuse to open them.

I recommend books by
Angela Davis
bell hooks
Audre Lorde
Kimberle Crenshaw
Brittney Cooper
to the pseudo-Pan Africanists entrenched
in psychobabble
claiming keys to Black liberation,
and block the diehards.

Do you remember
The Black Man's Guide to Understanding the Black Woman?
How that book spread around campus?

That passage in her book where she said
black women who ignore the black man's authority,
should be soundly slapped in the mouth?

Were you at the Spelman-Morehouse forum?
Air in the room heavy as a scud cloud,
my heart like a missile when I stood,
stammered and shook
as I argued Black women have supported Black men
since we arrived on these shores shackled together.
We soar in every profession there is,
and how dare a Black woman say a Black man
had any right to slap the face of a woman
who could be her sister?

Laura,
Umar Johnson
must have been absent the day
his psychology professor discussed displacement.

How much easier it is
to strike out
at Black women
than land a mighty blow
on the system trying to kill us both.

Sis, I imagine your face as you read this letter.
Shaking your head with all your Detroit swag.
Girl.Why do you care what he says?

Khari is a good man,
yet there are
kernels of guilt and fear
that I have not been enough,
buried beneath this anger
over misogynoir.

Mother to Mother

When you are black
and your hair is natural
you'd better keep your products in stock at home
because getting the good stuff
can be a problem after 8 at night.

I was in one of those stores
with a name that ends in -art
and
has Beyonce bombinating over the loudspeaker
but can't manage to stock
a decent moisturizing shampoo in the ethnic hair section.

A white woman joins me in the aisle:

Excuse me, but can I ask you a question?
Can you recommend an oil?
My son has dry hair and scalp.
I got him the Head and Shoulders but it wasn't helping.

It's probably too drying, I said.
Is his hair thick like, Black people's hair?

Yes, my husband is black.

How old is your son?
He's 17. He's a special needs child.
I have to do everything for him, or else he won't do it.

Get a little olive oil, I said.
Warm it on the stove, just until it's a little hot to the touch.
Take a cotton ball, run it all over his scalp, and let him sit for 10-15 minutes,
then he can wash his hair.
The oil should help lift the flaking off his scalp.
You can try Shea Moisture products for him.

Oh, thank you. I didn't know what to do.

It just sits there, like cradle cap.
I can't have him going around looking like that.

I understand, I said.

I wished I could have asked her husband,
his mother,
his sisters,
his aunts,
why
did they not ever teach this mother
what we do between washings

Come here baby,
let me fix that head

to sit him down between her knees,
cover his shoulders with a hand towel
gently part his hair with a wide-toothed comb,
scratch up the flaking,
rub oil between each part,
brush it neat.

Thank you, she said.
I didn't want you to think--

You're welcome, I said.
How else would you know unless you ask?

Volition

They don't want us,
anyone else,
to want it,
touch it.

Adjectives
like coarse,
leave scars, like
sandpaper on skin.

North Carolina:
sixteen-year-old black girl
in the center of a circle of her teammates

not to cheer
before running
on the softball field

but to cut every bead
out of her braids
for her to be allowed to play.

Arizona, Louisiana, Kentucky—
Black children beaming with
braids, locs, Afros, headwraps
forced out of class.

Had it been my son competing
in a wrestling tournament,
compelled to stand still
as a white woman
with thick scissors
severed his locs
it would have taken six security officers
to hold me back.

Sheep are sheared more kindly.

The Crown Act.
My Lord.
A law to let us be.

I was in love
with the soft tufts of my son's hair.

When he was eighteen months,
I coiled them around my finger,
but I stopped spinning them
because I wanted him to choose.

When he was 20, he came to me.

I want to loc my hair.

Three hours parting his thick Afro
half-inch square sections
fingertips burrowing into shea butter
enshrouding,
clockwise twisting
dozens of neat rows.

Two days later, he says,
"Thank you, but I don't like the way these locs look on me.
Can you take them out?"

I nod.
Softly unfurl the coils
with a comb.

Commencement

We stand.

Wrinkled gown
after wrinkled gown,
before we see Khari,
age 21,
perfectly pressed
gown and suit,
hair cut into a Caesar.

We cheer as he reaches over
to the aisle seat
to quickly hug Mom.

I do not move

as they announce awards,
the valedictorian and salutatorian
deliver their speeches,

as almost 600 graduates walk across the stage,
wave at families and friends,
shake hands as they receive their diplomas.

When they finally announce Khari's name,
and he rises,
walks to the podium,

I close my eyes

thank Daddy
Saundra
Aunt Joan
Grandma
Pop-Pop
Nana
Uncle Ralph
Uncle Reggie
Uncle Don

for watching over us.

I raise my arms towards Heaven,
thanking God
for so blessing
the work of my heart and hands,

because just the week before,

I almost swerved off the road when Khari says,

I am failing a couple of classes.
I am not going to finish my degree this spring.

I pulled over to a side street.
Turned around to face him,
my voice slapping each side of the car.

"What? Why not?
And why did you wait until now to tell me?"

I missed some classes and was late with some assignments.
I can still walk for graduation,
but I have to take two classes in the fall for my degree.

"And you better," I said.
"How will you get to campus?
You know I can't drive you!"

I will have to take a train and a couple of buses.

"And you will.
All that money I saved and that your grandparents left for you.
You will not miss another class or another assignment."

I will finish, Mom. I promise.

December 2015,
Khari earns his degree.

PART VII

WHY DIDN'T YOU TELL ME?

2016

I.

Three days since Khari returned from his college's music festival.
He has not slept.
Talks profusely and rapidly.

Noon. Khari's shift begins at two.
"Khari, aren't you going to be late?"
He vigorously waves me away.
Keeps talking on the phone with a friend
about his plans for his rap career.

"You seem really agitated since you got back from your trip.
Do you want me to get you some help,"
I gently ask once he gets off the phone.

No. Leave me alone!
You're always on my case.
I'm going over to Nana's.

I call Donna as soon as he leaves,
tell her Khari is on edge.
She assures me he can stay until he calms down.

Going to Mom's instead of work.
Something is wrong.

I call my co-worker who is a social worker.
She advises me to contact a crisis intervention team.
There is a 24-48 hour waiting period.

Donna calls me that night, a tremor in her voice.
"He's getting worse."
I grab my keys.
As I rush to Mom's, I dial 911.
Describe Khari's symptoms and request an ambulance.

Khari, usually friendly, cracking jokes,
is seated and frowning, rambling,
rocking back and forth in his chair,
hands tightly gripping the sides.

Nothing has been the same for this family since Pop-Pop died.
Nothing!

Ten minutes later, the doorbell rings.
Two police officers.

I think of Kenneth Chamberlin.
Pause before I pull the latch.
I open the screen door
but cannot let myself stand aside
until I have my say.

"My son is most likely manic depressive,
and he is not violent."
"Please," I say.

I cannot finish my thought aloud.
I lock eyes with the officer in front of me.

He and his partner are Latino.
Quiet nods,
as if they understood my plea not to hurt or shoot my son.
We go upstairs.

"What's going on?" the officers inquire.
They said, Khari points at us, *that I need help*.
The officers calmly invite Khari to go out to the ambulance.
Fine. I'll go.
My heart is racing,
knowing Khari is complying out of fear of the police.

Mom sits at her desk with her back to us,
head bowed,
shoulders shaking.
Donna follows us out to the ambulance.

As we wait to be seen
at our Local Public Hospital's
psychiatric emergency ward,
Khari, frowning, turns to me.

Men used to use you for sex. It's disgusting!

My cheeks run hot.
Never had a string of men.
The only man allowed to spend night was a boyfriend of three years.
He had been kind to Khari.

I didn't want anyone thinking I am promiscuous,
but I do not argue with Khari.

"Calm down," the officer says.
Khari is quiet.

Fear of the police.

Triage.
Khari must remove his clothes
down to his underwear,
surrender his shoes
and cell phone, put on a gown.

A corridor of rooms with clear glass windows
to wait until a psychiatrist interviews him.

This feels like jail.

For that hour and a half,
Khari's profanity bounces off the walls
as he rambles on about how our family
has not been the same since Daddy's death.

The doctor listens to Khari's ranting,
asks me to describe what I observed in Khari
over the last 24 hours,
determines that Khari is having a manic episode,
and must be admitted.

You're leaving me here? I can't believe it!

I look back at him as I am buzzed outside.
Khari stares at me with widened eyes.

His eyes.
His almond-shaped eyes were the first things I saw
in his ultrasound image.

I shudder at the fear on his face.

"I will be back tomorrow,"
I call out through the exit door,
and turn away so he does not see me cry.

Next day, Donna and I are back.
Everyone else in the waiting area scrolls through their phones,
flips through magazines, talks quietly,
as a woman screams behind the locked ward for 20 minutes.

What has been happening to my son since last night?

Once we are allowed to see Khari, he paces,
rocks back and forth in his chair,
tightly grips a pencil.

A social worker patiently explains the admission process.
Her soft tone puts me at ease, and I hug her,
hopeful Khari will receive compassionate care.

After I tell Khari's supervisors he is ill,
I speak with two of his college roommates.

They tell me about the music festival they attended with Khari,
how he ran onstage uninvited,
tore off his shirt,
grabbed the mic from the performers to hype up the audience and rap.

Many days during his junior and senior years,
Khari stayed in bed instead of going to class.

Now I knew why Khari missed so many classes,
why his college grades fluctuated so much.
He was depressed and none of us knew.

He finished his bachelor's degree out of love for me.

II.
Later that day, the hospital calls.
Orderlies tackled him the night before,
gave him a shot of risperidone.

My powerlessness nauseates me.
I try not to visualize Khari manhandled,
jabbed with a needle.

At our visit the next day,
Khari pulls out a chair for me,
and beckons for me to talk to him.

My eyes well at this sign of my son coming back to me.

During the ten days he in the hospital,
Donna and I visit almost every day.
Mom, Anike, my niece, our cousin Eric,
and four of Khari's friends see him too.

The lithium slurs his speech.
Makes him drool.
Khari insists nothing is wrong with him.
Nobody believes me, Khari weeps.

My heart shatters beneath a facade of courage.

We tell him he is loved, and we are here for him.

The next day, Khari gives me a drawing from art therapy.

Two sloppy circles
with two dots for eyes,
downturned mouths.

I want to come home.

Khari calls me multiple times every day.
How someone took a shit in a chair.
That he does not need to be in the hospital.

You need to check yourselves in here, see what it's like.
Check yourselves in here and deal with YOUR issues.

Khari tells me that one night he could not sleep,
and he asked a nurse if he could sit by her.
She yells at him to go back to his room.
I'm sure she was tired, but
I am devastated by this abrasive rebuff.

Khari makes friends.
Encourages patients to ask their doctors
for the names, descriptions, and side effects of their medications.

His advocacy for himself, other patients, makes me proud,
but the staff tells him to stop interfering with patient care.

After about a week, the hospital invites me
for a family meeting with a staff psychiatrist and social worker.
They give us the number to set up his outpatient care.

adjusting well to his medication
highly functional
obviously intelligent
So *important Khari take his lithium and risperidone,*
a*void alcohol and marijuana.*
People with bipolar disorder

can lead fulfilling, normal lives with proper care.

III.
Khari is home from the hospital.
Five of his friends come over to enjoy
a six pack of beer before they go out to eat.

The time to take his medication approaches.
I don't want to take that medication, he sneers,
and leaves with his friends.

Two weeks later, he stops his meds altogether.
The mania re-emerges.

I do not feel like teaching,
and I do not want to be home.

Khari is angry, agitated, berates me for calling the police
and having him hospitalized.

"I did not call the police," I protest.
"I dialed 911 and the police came to make sure the situation was safe."

I could have DIED!
I stare into his eyes.

"I would have jumped in front of you and caught the bullet."

I am afraid for Khari to leave the house.
He is unpredictable.

He goes to his old job,
refuses to leave the front entrance
until his friend gets off work.

His loses his wallet, wanders Columbus Circle,
and a few kind strangers
pay his bus fare to our neighborhood.

Khari sits outside all night.
Befriends a man that I find sitting in my living room
when I get home from work.
Six feet, husky, and barefoot.

"Khari," I say, as I pull him into my bedroom,
"if you don't get him out of here right now, I will."

The man is polite, and leaves after he finishes his pizza.
I take away Khari's house keys.
Secretly erase the man's number from his phone.
Mom stays with Khari during the day so I can go to work.

I break down in front of our secretary
as we weigh my options to get time off to care for
Khari without losing any pay.

Some of my students see me crying
as I am ushered into the bathroom
so I can collapse in peace.

Khari tells me he wants to die.

You don't understand.
This shit is hard!

I take Khari to the emergency psychiatric ward twice.
Both times, doctors determine he is not
an immediate danger
to himself or anyone else,
and send him back home with me.

One day Khari rants at us for ten hours.
I call the hospital psychiatrist in desperation.

"See if he will take one pill of risperidone."

After hours of begging, he does.
Fifteen minutes later, he bumps into the wall,
staggers into my room,
falls on my bed and passes out.

I stroke his face as he sleeps.

I love you, Khari.
I will never give up on you.

When I awaken, I hope for calm.
After eight hours of sleep, Khari opens his eyes.
And rants again.

Cousin Darryl gives me a deacon's phone number.
He is a psychiatrist in private practice.

It is important that your son receives continuity of care.
It often takes patients three to five years to manage their illness.

Three to five years?

I cannot do this, I say.

Yes. Yes you can.

IV.
Three weeks after his release,
Khari suffers a psychotic break.

Mom and I are taking Khari to pick up his new eyeglasses.
Before the bus comes, Khari is cursing and dancing around.

Mom despises profanity.
We both ask him to stop.

I'm doing this for y'all.

Mom turns red in the face, and I step between them.
"Mom, go home. Please. I've got him."

I pray we get his glasses without incident,
because Khari is talking about beating up
a man we know who abuses his wife.

Miraculously, Khari is calm in the eyeglass store,
but when we get home, Khari paces his room.
Looks at me. Smiles.

I'm going to kill your son.

I slip into my bedroom and call Donna.
Ask her to call for an ambulance.
"I am calling Brian to go to your house to calm him down," Donna pleads.
"Are you serious right now?" I exclaim.
I hold the phone close to Khari's room
so she hears him rave about doing himself in.

"Oh my, God!" Donna is crying. Hangs up to call for help.

"Take us to That Good Hospital. Please," I beg,
when the police and paramedics arrive.
To my surprise, the paramedics' supervisor approves.
It isn't in our borough.
Our Local Public Hospital is full, as are several others.
We are on our way to the best hospital network in New York.

God heard me.

Khari is there for three weeks.
The facility is clean.
Floor-to-ceiling windows usher a bevy of sunrays.
Art therapy. A live cellist in the evenings.
A rec area with a TV. Board games in the visiting room.
Dominoes. Connect Four, Scrabble on Khari's good days.
On a few bad days, Khari frowns at us and tells us to go home.

The psychiatrists prescribe Depakote and Zyprexa
instead of lithium and risperidone.

Much gentler, like the staff.

When Khari is loud and agitated,
they put him in a padded room until he de-escalates.
No jabs of a risperidone-filled needle.

Khari is scowling and gruff during the exit meeting,
as we discuss after-care at a community-based clinic,
with a psychiatric nurse and a therapist.
I am embarrassed by Khari's anger, but
they are understanding.
I thank and hug his doctors and social workers,
and they smile.

As I drive home,
the sun is bright.
Like my hope.

2017

I.

For a full year, Khari sleeps through most days.
Showers once or twice a week.

Medication slows him.
Khari gains almost a hundred pounds.

He rarely ventures beyond home, Mom's house,
the outpatient clinic.

I buy Khari a gym membership.
Encourage healthy well-balanced meals. Yoga.

I accompany Khari when he sees his psychiatric nurse.
She asks how is doing, how his job search is going.

There is no reason why you can't work.

She encourages the same lifestyle changes that I do.
Reminds him not to drink alcohol. It's a depressant.

If he must imbibe, just one beer.

Just one beer.

I wish his friends would listen.
Invite him to alcohol-free fun.

When they invite Khari out, they often go to bars.
I plead with Khari not to go with them or to refuse to drink.
I don't want to stand around not drinking. I won't have any fun.

I am exasperated, but I get it.
Khari wants to feel normal.

I am broken, he says.

"No, you're not!" I say every time.
"You have an illness. You are a warrior."

Depression captures me too.
I stop going out to dance or see friends as often as I had.

Sometimes I stare at the television,
mindlessly channel surf.

I confide in friends about Khari's challenging recovery.
They listen, even when they do not know what to say.

A sister-friend:
You completed your thesis for your second master's
while you worked full-time and supported your son on this
journey.

Trees give oxygen to every living thing,
and even they shed their leaves.
What makes you think you don't deserve rest?
Self-care?

I find out that my union offers free counseling.
I sign up.
That's good, another friend says.
I can't understand what you're going through.

During our six sessions,
my therapist assures me I am doing all I can for Khari.
It helps.

II.
Tanya and I plan a showcase at the Nuyorican,
for my first three books of poetry, and her first.
Khari offers to be our MC.
He is tentative at first,

but when he announces me —*my mom, Carla Cherry*!
I hear pride when he calls my name.
He smiles as we pose for pictures.

A bloom of Amaryllis.

III.
I think of Khari's father.
How he felt when he was diagnosed,
the way he struggled to hold on to jobs,

whether he ever tried medication,
ever felt broken,
was ashamed.

I sow a seed of forgiveness.
It sprouts.

2018

I.
Khari shows interest in working.
Sometimes he goes off his medication for a bit but resumes.

The nurse convinces him to take a small dose of Wellbutrin.
Khari gets an unpaid internship and sees his friends regularly.

The National Alliance on Mental Illness.

I join a local chapter.
Attend a support group.

Parents share how their young adults
struggle to work steadily,
refuse psychiatric support,
disappear,
or go to jail.

I count our blessings.

I raise several hundred dollars for N.A.M.I.-Walk NYC.

As we walk toward the Brooklyn Bridge,
we share stories.

I meet other family members and friends
of people living with mental illness.

One man near Khari's age
tells me he has bipolar disorder,
and he is working through it.
I shake his hand.

It is drizzling.
Sunrays part the clouds like curtains.

II.
I have neither
the strength,
nor words
to write a poem
that can convey
what was done to our family
when Donna
found a lumpy growth in her right hip.

She first suspected it was from
her many hours
cross-legged on her bed,
proofing manuscripts.

She can barely eat.
An MRI.

Worst case of synovial cell sarcoma
the doctor has seen in 18 years of practice.
Liver and kidney failure.

She is admitted to The Good Hospital.

An eleven-hour surgery
to remove the tumor from her right leg.

It leaves a hole big enough
for two fingers
and it never closes.

Dialysis.
Metastasis.

For five months,
we are at her side in the hospital,
three to eight hours,
almost every day.

When she asks one of us
to spend the night with her
on one of her last wakeful nights
in hospice,

we are spent.
Khari is the one who stays.

Donna passes away
three months before her 45th birthday.

It takes Khari nine months to cry.

2019

Khari gets a full-time job.
He likes it at first but struggles with setting a sleep schedule.

I often must wake him,
or Mom will call him to make sure he is up.

Khari survives the probationary period,
secures his own health insurance.

Khari socializes with his co-workers more than he works,
is warned several times about attendance and job performance.

Frustrated, I do research to understand—
distractibility, talkativeness, impulsiveness
are common with bipolar disorder.

I focus on the positive signs:
        therapy engagement
        voluntary medication compliance.
        Khari gives me money towards the bills.
        Cooks for himself.
        He is dating.
        She is pretty, smart, and headed to graduate school.
        Khari talks about moving out.

2020

I.
COVID-19.
Remote work.

Increased disenchantment with his job.
Without face-to-face socialization with his coworkers
Khari is increasingly disconnected from his job duties.

> In my underwear, freshly awakened,
> worried by silence in Khari's room,
> I knock on his door.

He is still asleep, and it is already after 7:30 a.m.
I rouse him.
He mumbles that he will get up but does not.

Rage and anxiety swirl around me.
I am a tornado.

I snatch his cell phone out of his bed.
"I am taking back this phone!"

> Khari jumps out of bed.
> *Give me back my phone!*

> "No!" I scream.

He storms into my bedroom,
tries to pry it from my hands.

For five minutes, we wrestle.
Me, 5'8.
Khari, 6 feet,
22 years younger.

I gasp for breath.

Khari, whether he wants to avoid hurting me or exhaustion,
extricates himself from me.

Goes into his room.
His cell phone is still in my hand.
This victory is an empty, hollow room.

I decide to give Khari space.

*It can take three to five years for people with mental illness to manage it
upon first diagnosis.*
You can do this.

I do not protest much
when Khari quits his job shortly thereafter.

II.
After Khari's 26th birthday,
he is disconnected from his outpatient provider.
They stopped seeing clients beyond that age.

Continuity of care.

The new provider Khari finds,
does the intake procedure,
and never gives him an appointment.

Psychiatric and therapy is done virtually.
Pandemic.

Khari finishes the medication he got
from his original provider,
then stops taking medication altogether.

I encourage Khari to seek a new psychiatric clinic,
but he refuses.

All you do is worry about me taking medication.
You never trust me to work this out myself.
What else can a therapist tell me?
I have my friends to talk to.
I am fine.

I want to swoop in.
Fix things, but I step back.

I monitor Khari for signs of mania,
severe depression,
or psychosis.

Over the course of ten unmedicated months,
Khari is calm.
Reads books or plays video games to pass the time.

A friend who lives with bipolar disorder
says Khari appears to be in remission,
but should seek psychiatric outpatient care
to avoid a bipolar relapse.

III.
This world tells us to hold our breath,
suck in our stomachs.

Bury problems and frustration
deep in the diaphragm.

Get the job done.

I give myself the greatest gift,
and share Khari's story with strangers.

A fellow teacher at a Regents grading session tells a joke—
at his college, one only needed to pay half their room and board
if you had a schizophrenic roommate. He laughs to himself.

If I curse him out, I will miss out on per session pay.
If I slap him, I will get arrested.

I push away from our table, slam my papers on an empty one.
Refuse to speak.

At lunch with the other teachers at our table,
I tell them how I feel about the joke, and why.

It is the first time I tell any neurotypical people
outside my circle about Khari's illness.

Listening ears and empathy are upwash.
My angst, out to sea.

I tell trusted co-workers and acquaintances.
I hear their personal experiences with mental illness,
their children, relatives, or friends, who live with mental illness.

My inner circle expands into a ring of healing.

2021

I.

Khari's new psychiatric nurse diagnoses him with ADHD.
How is that possible, I ask myself.

I never saw any signs of it while he was growing up.
This provider is the expert,
Khari is an adult, so I relent.

He prescribes Strattera for Khari.

Khari has a job that he loves.
He is on time and excelling.

After two months, he is erratic.
Tells me he feels like his heart is racing.

We go to the hospital.
They listen to his symptoms, run tests.

The hospital has no room in its psych ward.
Because he is not a danger to himself or anyone else,
he is sent home, encouraged to follow up with his provider.

Two weeks later,
mania and paranoia.

He tells his nurse he wants cannabis
instead of psychiatric drugs.

The nurse tells him no,
so Khari says he will find someone who will approve.

Khari wakes me up for midnight walk.

Shhh!! You hear that?

Passes me a folded-up note:

I know it's off the books.
Nowhere is going to be safe.
Trust no one, especially white people.

Khari does not sleep.
Calls friends and family all hours of the night.

I have ADHD.
I'm a genius, and they've been holding me back!

He takes multiple IQ tests to show us all!

I am afraid to leave Khari alone.

We find a new provider who agrees to work with Khari,
but he first must be stabilized.

Back to the hospital
for the first time in five years.

In triage, Khari paces the floor. Raps loudly.
Wide-eyed look when I hug him goodbye.

The phone rings the next morning.

Your son was not getting good psychiatric care.
Patients with bipolar disorder should not be on Strattera.
It is a stimulant.
It triggers mania.

Three weeks in another hospital.
The staff is nice, but the ward is old.

No floor-to-ceiling windows,
flood of sunrays.

I am daunted

by malodors of old meat and cheese.

Khari is irate that he is there.
Phone calls at least ten times a day begging to come home.

Before Khari's release, I clean Khari's room.

To atone for deprivation of sky and sun,
I have his walls repainted cerulean blue.

I call a family friend who is an attorney
so we can sue Khari's psychiatric nurse.

He instructs me to find a doctor
willing to testify so he can begin the paperwork.

Khari does not want to engage the process.

I respect his wish for four months,
but Khari's depression feeds my wrath.

I call Big-Name-Law-Firm for a consultation.

I'm not saying your son
did not experience malpractice
but his case does not meet our criteria for taking it on.
I am sorry.

So, there is nothing I can do because
Khari is not catatonic or dead.
Or maybe the case will not make enough money.

That this provider
will not be held responsible
stokes embers of rage that smolder.
Spread.
I contemplate murder.

II.
Mom,
how come you never told me?

Told you what?

About my father's bipolar disorder.
Why didn't you warn me?

I was too afraid to say it.
Did not know how.

Clung to hope,
love,
and The Oracle.

Thought *the help* would be easier.

2022

I.
Khari is stable.
Taking his meds.
Looking for the right fit for work.
Saving money for his someday.

I am still a helicopter mother.

I hover,

swoop in,
ask how he is doing,
swoop out,
revel in
family and friends,
teaching and writing,

but sometimes

I am out of trim,
must straighten out,
sail smoothly on the wind.

Aided and abetted by social media,
comparison stalks us both--

the scholastics, careers, coupling, parenthood, of his friends,
children of contemporaries.

On the days I am happy for them,
sad for us,
I think of Roman 12:6:

Having then gifts differing according to the grace that is given to us, let us use them.

I put the expectations I had for Khari's lifepath
in a hope chest.

Set it on fire.

I write an essay
about the need for non-police response to mental health crises,
the work we are doing to *thrive* with bipolar disorder.
I show it to Khari,
ask for permission to share it
with my Nonfiction Creative Writing class.

Why didn't you use my real name?
"I wanted to protect your privacy."

Isn't the point of your essay to help eliminate the stigma?

I submit the piece to *Raising Mothers.*
It is published.

I post it online.
Hundreds of encouraging words.

You are so brave.

Sometimes.

Khari
is the one.

II.
Khari sits next to me.

I just finished reading your book.
It was a hard read, especially about my dad.
And you worked so hard to send me to college,
even though I never really wanted to go.

"Why didn't you tell me?"
We look at each other and laugh.

I get it. I didn't really have a solid plan for my life after high school.

He pauses.
Did I really say men use you for sex the first time I was hospitalized?

"I know it was the mania.
The few boyfriends I had good hearts, but they were not right for me."

You're about to get back out there, right?

"Yes. I am talking to God, praying for my soulmate, taking my time."

Khari puts his arm around me,
and pats my knee.

Mom, thanks for everything.
Try not to worry so much about me.
I'll figure it out.

I lean on his shoulder.

I am praying for you, son,
planting seeds of hope every season.

Here for you if you need.
Just ask.

We will hold hands.

I will follow you,
stepping
stone
to stone.

Afterword

May He Bless My Name emerged from a request from another poet in 2017 that I write a poem about motherhood, and it became my thesis for my MFA in Creative Writing at the City College of New York.

I am incredibly grateful to:

Khari for permitting me to share our story,

my family for their never-ending support,

David Groff, for being my thesis advisor and encouraging me to push my work,

my fellow poets in the Academy for Teachers Poetry Group and the Informal Poetry Workshop for their critiques of many of the poems in this volume,

Dr. Tanya Manning-Yarde and Rosebud Ben-Oni for generously reading this manuscript and providing invaluable, honest feedback,

Anthony Langhorne, president of iiPublishing, for always believing in my writing,

and to everyone who generously purchases and reads this book.

May it serve as a source of discussion, hope, and inspiration.

OTHER WORK
BY CARLA M. CHERRY

ii Publishing
Gnat Feathers and Butterfly Wings
Thirty Dollars and a Bowl of Soup
Honeysuckle Me
These Pearls Are Real
Stardust and Skin

Grandma Moses Press
Clap Your Hands, Stomp Your Feet

Finishing Line Press
Sundays and Hot Buttered Rolls: A Granddaughter of Harlem Speaks

Carla M. Cherry is a veteran high school English teacher. Her work has appeared in various publications, including Random Sample Review, Anti-Heroin Chic, 433, and Raising Mothers. A Best of the Net and Pushcart Prize nominee, her five books of poetry, Gnat Feathers and Butterfly Wings, Thirty Dollars and a Bowl of Soup, Honeysuckle Me, These Pearls Are Real, and Stardust and Skin are available via iiPublishing. Carla authored two chapbooks, Clap Your Hands, Stomp Your Feet (Grandma Moses Press) and Sundays and Hot Buttered Rolls: A Granddaughter of Harlem Speaks (Finishing Line Press). She holds an M.F.A. in Creative Writing from the City College of New York.

www.ingramcontent.com/pod-product-compliance
Lightning Source LLC
Chambersburg PA
CBHW060909120626
46553CB00001B/262